Water Gardening

Water Gardening

By JACK KRAMER

Pools, Fountains and Plants

Botanical Plates by MICHAEL VALDEZ
How-to Drawings by ADRIAN MARTINEZ

CHARLES SCRIBNER'S SONS
New York

A-7.71 [MH]

Printed in the United States of America
SBN 684-12414-9 (trade cloth)
SBN 684-12415-7 (trade paper)
Library of Congress Catalog Card Number 76-143916

ACKNOWLEDGMENTS

My sincere thanks to the people at Van Ness Water Gardens for answering many of my questions and for supplying photos of water lilies. My gratitude also goes to Clint Bryant for expediting photos in amazing speed, and to my very patient artists Michael Valdez and Adrian Martinez.

Mr. Valdez personally trekked through the large water gardens of the Oakland Museum, knee deep in water, to draw plants and further kept many specimens alive (to his amazement and mine) in the bathtub of his tiny apartment in San Francisco.

Personal thanks to the fine people at the Oakland Museum of Oakland, California who allowed us to enter their water gardens and gave us their fullest cooperation.

I also wish to thank Longue Vue Gardens of New Orleans, La., Rosedown Plantation and Gardens of St. Francisville, La. and the General Electric Company for contributing photos to this work.

Contents

Introduction: An Old Art for New Garden Beauty

Water as a decorative element has been part of many gardens of the past. In fresco paintings of the Egyptian dynasties (1225 B.C.) ponds and canals and cultivation of exotic water plants were part of the theme. The earliest garden designers of China and India were quick to realize the beauty of Lotus pools in their landscapes, and in ancient Japanese gardens water was a dominant feature. Spain is famous for its water gardens where many fine patios include a fountain or pool to make a cool secluded retreat.

Water in the garden—reflecting pools, ponds, fountains, and waterfalls, are desirable in almost any garden, large or small. Water brings tranquility, repose, motion, and sound to the setting. What is more soothing to the ear than the quiet trickle of a fountain on a hot day? What is more satisfying to the eye than reflections of sky and trees in a small pond where moving shadows present an everchanging picture? And finally, water in the landscape opens a new avenue of gardening—the cultivation of exotic water lilies, lotus, hyacinths and other aquatic plants.

Where once pond and pool housings were cumbersome and expensive, today we have prefabricated pools—plastic, stone, fiberglass—to sink into the ground. For the do-it-yourselfers there are metal tanks, photographers' trays, old laundry tubs and even Chinese fry pans that can become a water accent in one afternoon. While many of these are not deep enough for water lilies, they are adequate for many charming aquatics. Fountains with pumps to keep water in motion are more sophisticated and less expensive than even a few years ago. New materials and methods have made water gardening easy.

The avenues of water gardening are many; the setting can be a simple landscape with a reflecting pool, or a traditional pool where you can grow lovely water lilies, or it might be a more elaborate feature such as a fountain or waterfall. These decorative accents are now available to most people where formerly they were only in gardens of the wealthy.

There is an exciting new kind of gardening waiting for you when water becomes a part of your property. There are plants for in the pool such as lotus, water hawthorn, and water lilies. Around the pool, you can grow Egyptian paper plant, arrowhead, plantain lily and iris and there are floating plants such as hyacinth and azolla. There are hundreds of lovely aquatics but unfortunately little information on how to grow them or what to grow them in.

This book I hope, will fill the void and provide ample information on plants and pools, fountains, and waterfalls, and how to build them inexpensively. This is a present-day treatment of an ancient art; yesterday's beauty is at your fingertips today with water gardening.

Jack Kramer

1. Water As a Decorative Element

A natural stream or running brook in a setting is indeed beautiful; even the most hardened nongardener is attracted to it. But even though few properties are blessed with this water accent, landscapes do not have to be all greenery. Today there is a wide selection of prefabricated and custom pools to make property unique.

The addition of a shimmering sheet of silver to the usual green scene complete the natural marriage of water and plants. A blanket of lovely flowers and a verdant lawn are prizes indeed but the garden becomes a treasure when a pool brimming with colorful water lilies or lotus flowers is introduced into the plan.

The water garden can be a concrete dish on a bed of crushed rock or a small cast-stone bowl at the end of a patio bench. It might be a submerged laundry tank, plastic tub, or metal dish. It may even be an impressive formal pool or an informal pond. Large or small, prefabricated or custom-made, metal or stone, submerged or elevated, the pool can be a lovely source of nearby nature whether used for aquatic plants or as a reflecting surface. And the water accent need not be expensive; there are pools to fit all budgets.

For those handy with tools, there are limitless ways to make dishes and water shells. Small cast-concrete dishes to hold water can be made in almost any shape; mosaic and aggregate containers are other possibilities.

For the gardener, the opportunity to grow lovely aquatics is a special kind of joy. These beautiful plants offer great satisfaction for little care: once the pool and plants are established, there is a bounty

A small concrete formal pool with stepping stones is a charming addition to this garden area. Note the graceful Cyperus grown in a tub in the center of the pool. (Calif. Association of Nurserymen photo)

of colorful blooms (there are no special tricks or secrets involved in the fascinating hobby of growing water plants.)

Waterfalls, cascades, and fountains—now in many designs—are more elaborate but still affordable ways to introduce water into the garden; these may be simple or complex depending upon your budget and site.

The Water Garden

Practically any property has space for water because pools come in enough sizes and materials to blend with almost any setting. In general, there are three types of pools: prefabricated dishes and bowls from nurseries or suppliers; made-to-order traditional formal pools with straight walls and geometrical designs; and the natural informal pool or pond with sweeping lines and a curved bottom.

Some pools are made of molded resin or fiberglass. These one-piece shells are set into a depression in the soil, filled with water, and edged with plants. This is an easy way to have an inexpensive pool in one afternoon. (See Chap. 4.) Of the same concept (but somewhat less expensive) is a large sheet of polyethylene plastic; it comes in a kit, with a metal edging strip. The plastic is laid in the hole and anchored with the metal. Most of these pools are desirable but they do have their limits. They are generally not deep or large enough for exotic water lilies or goldfish, but they can be lovely reflecting surfaces for trees and sky, or they can be embellished with floating plants. (There are only a few water lilies for the shallow pool; see Chap. 9.)

Prefabricated pools and dishes are available in several materials—stone aggregate, fiberglass, metal—that withstand weather and freezing. They can be put in place easily in one day. Use these small water

This fine informal pool is a shimmering sheet of water reflecting the hillside. A redwood island deck provides access to the scene. (Author photo)

Rocks and plants adorn this small formal concrete pool; the water is an integral part of this garden room. (Hedrich Blessing photo)

areas as a garden accent rather than as a feature. Put them near patios or paths where they are easily seen. If they are elevated, they will need background plantings. Submerged, they need aquatics to make them effective; grasses, water iris, and cannas will help to blend them into the landscape. A frame of finely crushed gravel is handsome too, or use ground covers such as Helxine (baby's tears) or Chamomile.

Salvaged items such as laundry tubs, metal tanks, kegs, and sawed barrels can also be used as pools, providing they are watertight. The small pool (less than 18 inches in diameter) has the advantage of being movable if it does not seem suitable in one place. Salvaged containers, like prefabricated dishes, should be used solely as accent.

Water and Its Place in the Landscape

First consider the pool's place and function. Will it be a viewing pool, with a small fountain, a reflecting pool, or a showplace for water plants? Decide first, and then select the appropriate kind of pool.

The traditional formal pool is expensive (unless you do most of the work) but naturally more satisfying. Formal pools are either sunken and bordered with stone or tile or walled, with seating ledges.

Design is of the utmost importance for the formal pool; it depends on simple, clean lines for its beauty. The rectangular shape is the most popular but elliptically and geometrically shaped pools are also desirable. Size and depth are other considerations and are discussed in Chap. 3.

A pair of concrete aggregate pools is a garden feature; rough edges of the pool are hidden in ground cover. (Calif. Association of Nurserymen)

A sawn-off barrel is home for these water plants; provides a spot of water in the landscape. (Author photo)

Informal pools need space to make them look natural (and natural they must be). Because of their irregular shape they must appear as though they have always been part of the garden plan. They should be framed with lush plantings and handsome rocks or stones.

In the large and deep pool it will be hard to resist growing water lilies; these are exciting plants that put on a stunning show. Other water plants are equally handsome and can certainly add color and form to any pool. Remember to put the pool in a sunny place if you want to grow aquatics: only full sunlight develops the plants to perfection.

Left: *A commercial dish is part of this water fountain; colorful flowers border the pool.* (Hedrich Blessing photo)

2. Dishes and Bowls for Pools

Small prefabricated dishes and bowls are popular because they are inexpensive, come in many sizes and materials, and can be installed easily. Buckets and tubs (usually fiberglass) for water lily growing are also at suppliers and can be placed in the ground or above the ground. They are 24 inches in diameter, 20 inches deep and accommodate one or two lilies.

Prefabricated Dishes and Bowls

Water containers—dishes and bowls—are available at nurseries and range up to 24 inches in diameter. They are made of metal, plastic, fiberglass, or concrete aggregate. Basically, they are water accents rather than water gardens because they are not deep enough for most plants.

Placement of these pools is important: when sunk in the ground they almost always need a frame of lush plants or else they appear as afterthoughts rather than as natural embellishments. Dishes or bowls can also be above ground level on a bench or at the end of a table where they will offer a silver reflection of sky and trees, a dramatic decoration.

In general, place dishes near the patio or terrace or walkway and path rather than out in the garden (here a traditional pool is more in harmony with the total setting). Small gardens rarely need an outlet pipe for drainage or an overflow pipe; the soil around the pool soaks up excess water. To change the water, hose the dish gently for a few minutes.

Pavings or edgings are not necessary; they bring too much atten-

A simple architectural dish is the water accent in this picture; it can be placed almost anywhere in the garden. (Architectural Pottery photo)

tion to the size of the water area. The main advantage of the small pool is its portability; it can be easily moved.

Salvaged pool forms are in the same class as prefabricated dishes and bowls and include old laundry tubs, tank ends, plastic bubbles, furnace ducts, oil drums, wine barrels, birdbaths without pedestals—almost anything that will hold water. These containers are effective when sunk in the ground to their rims, with gravel or ground cover as a frame. Like the commercial dishes, they generally are not large enough for water lilies or goldfish.

Do-It-Yourself Small Pools

Cast-concrete pools are fun to make and look good in the garden. Forms for the dish can be made or found. The curves of the two parts

The corner of this garden has a concrete aggregate pool surrounded by lush plantings and flowers. (Author photo)

Rigid plastic is the material for this dish pool; the frame of vertical plants is a perfect foil for the water accent. (Clint Bryant photo)

Old barrels make great water gardens; several different kinds of plants are in the pool. (Author photo)

of the form must be similar and be of a hard material; metal or wood does the job when the facing parts are brushed with a lubricant. The bottom pan holds the concrete mixture, and the top pan sets the mold; clamps at the edges hold the forms together firmly. Trim away concrete excess at the edges, and weight down the top form with brick or rubble. After the concrete sets (about two days) the bottom form is removed; the inner form is left in place as insurance against cracking. Wrap the bowl in burlap, and keep it damp for several days so that the concrete cures properly.

Other circular pools can be sand cast. At the bottom of the form, a rod is the axis on which a wooden template revolves. This revolving template forms the sand and the pool. First mold the damp sand and put in the concrete and smooth it against the sand walls. Add wire mesh, and cover with more concrete. Trowel the mix in place, and use a template to achieve the final surface for the bowl. Use cement, sand, and Haydite for the bowl.

Bucket and Tub Water Gardens

These are generally used as miniature water lily pools; they are made of tough fiberglass and last several years. The maximum size is

24 inches at the top tapering to 20 inches at the bottom and 20 inches deep. The bucket will hold one or two lilies.

For gardeners who admire and want water lilies but do not want to go through the work involved in the construction of a formal or informal custom pool, the tub garden is an ideal container. It can merely be placed on the ground, and filled with 8- to 10-inches of soil. The ideal depth of water over the crowns of the plant is from 8 to 10 inches.

Here, prefabricated dishes are used in a water cascade arrangement. Rocks set off the pool. (Clint Bryant photo)

On a pedestal, this architectural dish is a small but desirable spot of water in the garden. (Architectural Pottery Co. photo)

Pygmae lilies are especially suitable for the tub garden and include the Lydekeris types. Some good hardy lilies are: Gloriosa, White Laydekeri, Aurora, Joanne Pring and Carmine Laydekeri. If you want to try tropical lilies, plant Blue pygmae, Royal Purple or Zanzibar Blue.

Other plants for tub garden are water poppy and water snowflake. These do best planted in water from 5-to-6 inches deep and in 6-inches of soil or more.

3. *The Formal Garden Pool*

A pool, besides being decorative, affords a big bonus: it opens the door to the world of water plants. And who can really resist the bright exotic water lilies and lotus? Although an ancient art, growing water plants deserves more attention from today's gardener for it is a satisfying, exciting, and easy way to have lovely flowers.

Traditional or Formal Pools

A portable pool can be charming, but the formal pool is dramatic and becomes the center interest for the rest of the garden (in most cases, a water garden, for nothing is lovelier than exotic summer aquatics.)

When we think of Europe's great gardens, we also think of their spectacular pools: the French chateaux with their lovely water gardens, for example. The circular or rectangular pools of the Victorian era were slightly elevated and usually in the center of the garden plan, surrounded by walks and paths, and had elaborate fountains. Those grand gardens were lovely but are impossible to maintain today. Still, the idea and beauty behind the pools of yesteryear are as good as ever and perhaps more needed now, since beauty is steadily diminishing.

The traditional pool is rarely inexpensive, but it is not exorbitant, and it increases property value. The enterprising gardener will be able to construct his own pool at a moderate cost; other gardeners will need professional help.

A pool is permanent and is going to remain for the life of the house, so choose its location carefully. Make sketches of it on the

This formal pool is partially surrounded with brick paving; the water accent is handsomely landscaped with background plantings. (Clint Bryant photo)

landscape plan; it should be part of the total look. Incorporate it into a corner of a terrace or at the end of a path, and do put it where it can be seen from the house so that you can enjoy its beauty. If the pool is to adjoin a terrace, try to unite them by running the same type of paving around the pool edges. Be wary of placing the pool in the center of the terrace; to integrate it into the garden plan calls for clever landscaping with pot plants.

Find a sunny spot for the pool as most water plants need at least a few hours of daily sun. Avoid locations under trees; leaves decomposing in water are a bother to remove from the pool and when decomposed, create noxious gases that can harm fish and plants. Select a level site so that extensive excavating is not necessary.

Perspective

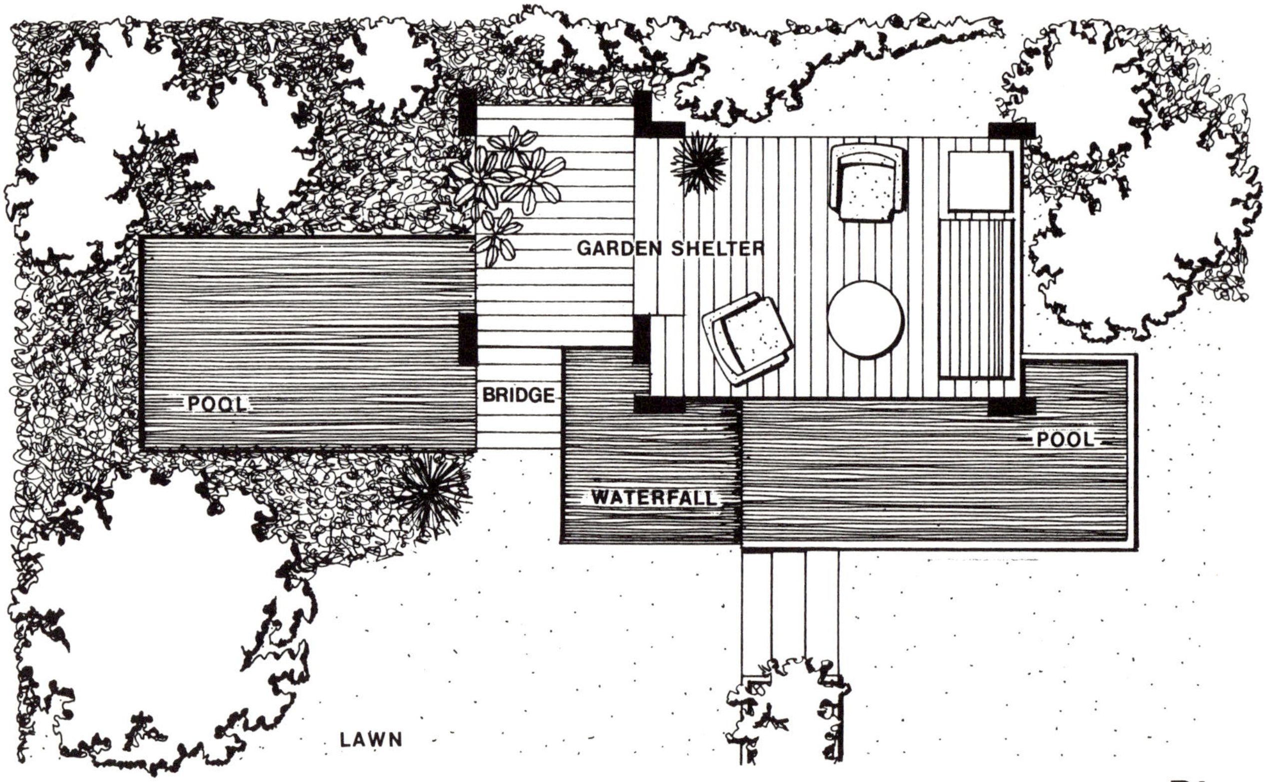

Plan

RECTILINEAR POOL DESIGN: ADRIÁN MARTÍNEZ

Generally, the formal pool is geometric in shape—rectangular, square or oblong—and is well suited to a terrace or patio that is also square or rectangular. Be sure the size of the pool is in scale with its surroundings; if the terrace is 20 x 30 feet, the pool should be approximately 5 x 8 feet for good balance. Avoid crowding as it ruins the effect.

Building the Pool

There are many building materials for pools, but concrete is perhaps the best. A concrete pool is easy and inexpensive to build, and easy to plant and clean. More important, once completed it is almost maintenance-free.

Brick is lovely and blends well with outdoor settings, but a brick pool can cause trouble. Even a well-laid brick wall will need two coatings of commercial waterproofing, and this is no guarantee against leaks. If you like the appearance of brick, trim the edges of the pool with it (or make a raised pool with brick walls) rather than using it for the shell.

Pools made of concrete block require the skill of an experienced mason. Even tightly sealed concrete-block walls are inferior to concrete in their ability to hold water. The greater size of the block means fewer mortar joints per square foot of surface, and although the walls are easier to reinforce than brick (because of their hollow cores), you will still have trouble with them.

The ideal depth for a small pool is about 24 inches. This allows a planting depth of 8 inches of soil, 12 inches of water to cover the crowns of plants, and a few spare inches. A pool filled to the top is not as handsome as one filled within a few inches of the top.

Digging the hole is hard work; try to hire someone to do it. For a 24-inch depth of water, excavate to 36 inches, allowing for a 6-inch bed of cinders and a 6-inch concrete floor. Be sure the cinders are really firmly in place and level; an irregular bed will cause cracks to develop in the floor. Line the floor with steel rods or wire mesh; the reinforcing material can be held in place with stones, if necessary.

A good basic concrete mix for pools consists of 1 part cement, 2 parts sand, and 4 parts aggregate (small stones). Rent a mixer from a supplier, or if you prefer, mixing can be done on a large board (this is hard work so be prepared). You can order ready-mixed concrete from dealers; the pour can be done in a few hours. (See Chap. 6.)

The pool floor is poured first. Gently put the concrete in place; do not throw it or it will separate. Tamp down the concrete very carefully at the corners and where the walls will be to the outer edges of the excavation. If the reinforcing material is dislodged by the weight of the concrete, set it back in place in the wet cement. When the pouring is over, smooth the concrete with a wooden board or a float. If you decide to use pipe lines for drainage, put them in place before any concrete is poured.

The walls of a pool also must be 6 inches thick. In an 8 x 10 foot pool, 2 feet deep, the water mass weighs close to 5 tons—a formidable weight that needs ample support. Wooden forms are necessary for the walls. You can construct your own, but it takes a great deal of time; it is easier to rent them from a supplier. Hold the forms in place with 2 x 4-feet supports. Check them with a level to be sure that they are straight and treat the forms with a lubricating oil so that they will be easy to pull away from the concrete.

Pool walls, like floors, need reinforcing with wire mesh or steel rods. Thrust the mesh into the wall forms; set them horizontally in the wet concrete as the pouring progresses. If you use steel rods, plunge them into the ground before the concrete is poured. Pour concrete into wooden forms evenly all around the pool. Do not fill one section and then the next; work around the pool. As you fill the forms make sure that the concrete is well tamped down where the walls meet the floor; most pools leak at these spots. Finish off the top surface of the walls with a wooden board or a float as soon as the concrete begins to set.

Let the concrete set for 48 hours before you remove the forms. Concrete hardens by setting, not by drying, so protect it from the drying action of sun and wind. Keep all surfaces covered with burlap or straw, and moisten the materials with sprinklings for about 10 days.

To make a plant shelf around the pool, bring the cement walls and the wooden framework to within 8 to 10 inches of the surface of the ground, and then take out the soil to form a shelf in back of the main walls. Dig down to provide a ridge; this ridge prevents the soil on the

A. Below–grade pool

1 MAKE HOLE LARGER THAN DESIRED SIZE, WET & TAMP DIRT

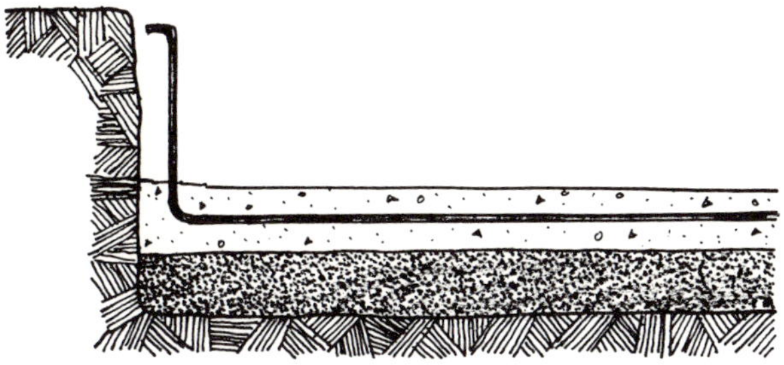

2 CINDERS OPTIONAL, POUR CONCRETE FLOOR WITH REINFORCING

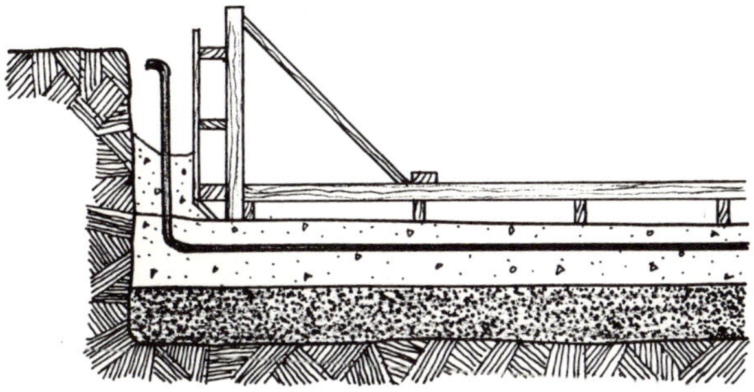

3 SET INSIDE FORMS, BRACING AGAINST OPPOSITE SIDE, POUR CONCRETE WALLS, TAMP WELL

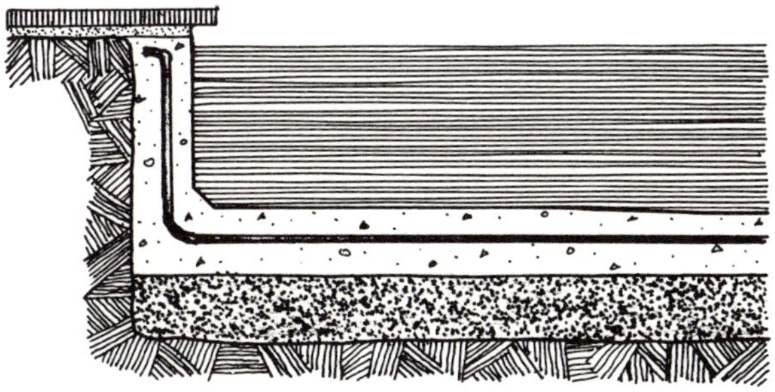

4 FINISH POUR, CURE & SEAL CONCRETE–EDGE OR CAP

B. Above–grade pool

1 SET OUTSIDE FORMS TO MAXIMUM SIZE, WET & TAMP DIRT

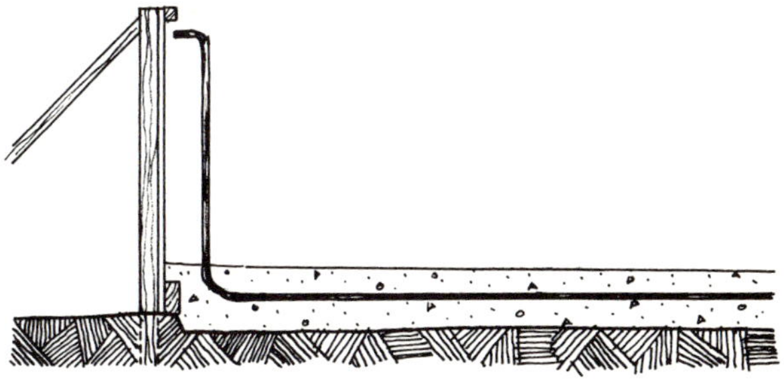

2 POUR CONCRETE FLOOR WITH REINFORCING

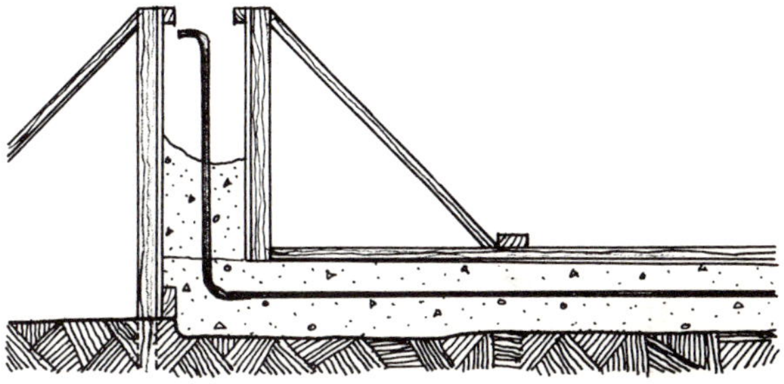

3 SET INSIDE FORMS, BRACING AGAINST OPPOSITE SIDE, POUR WALLS, TAMP WELL

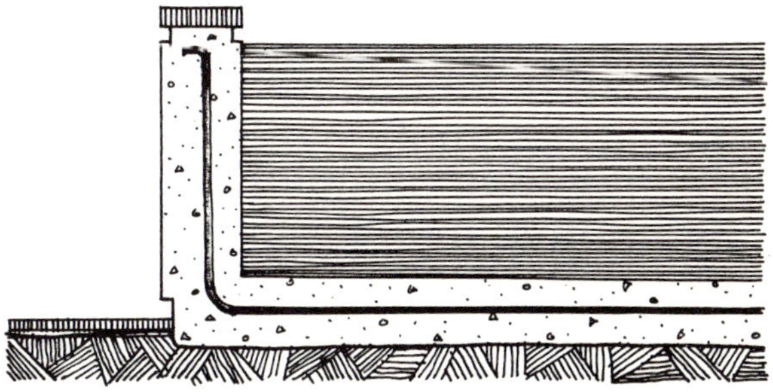

4 FINISH POUR, CURE & SEAL–CAP EDGES

WOODEN FORM POOL CONSTRUCTION

ADRIÁN MARTÍNEZ

shelf from falling into the pool. Make the shelf about 12 to 15 inches wide. You will need a short retaining wall in back of the soil to hold it in place; install narrow wooden supports to hold the cement until it sets. When the pool is filled, water will naturally flow over into the soil in the shelf for plants that like wet feet.

Freshly poured concrete walls and floors contain lime that is harmful to plants and fish, so a curing process is necessary.

Curing the Pool

Curing is the process of eliminating the lime content in the new concrete. There are many ways of curing; perhaps not the easiest but the best way is to:

1. Fill the pool with water, and let it stand 5 days.
2. Drain and refill the pool, and let the water stand 5 days.
3. Drain the pool again.
4. With 1 quart vinegar to 10 quarts water, scrub all the pool parts with a wire brush.
5. Hose down the pool with a strong spray of water.

At suppliers you will find chemical solutions to speed this process if time is important.

Painting the pool will not seal off the free lime because eventually the paint will deteriorate. If you want to paint the pool for esthetic reasons do it after the pool is cured. The paint will stick better and last longer on chemically neutral concrete. Use masonry latex or epoxy paint for the walls.

Brick walls and those made of concrete blocks will need two applications of commercial waterproofing compounds to seal them properly.

Drainage and Overflow

If you do not want to bother laying drain pipe, small pools can be emptied in various ways. Use a hose to siphon out water to a lower location where the water can evaporate in a storm sewer or gutter. Fill the hose with water, double over the ends, and put it into a siphoning position. It will take several hours to empty the pool.

Another method is to use an ordinary lead pipe that is fitted over the soil bed and plugged with a stopper or cork that can be removed

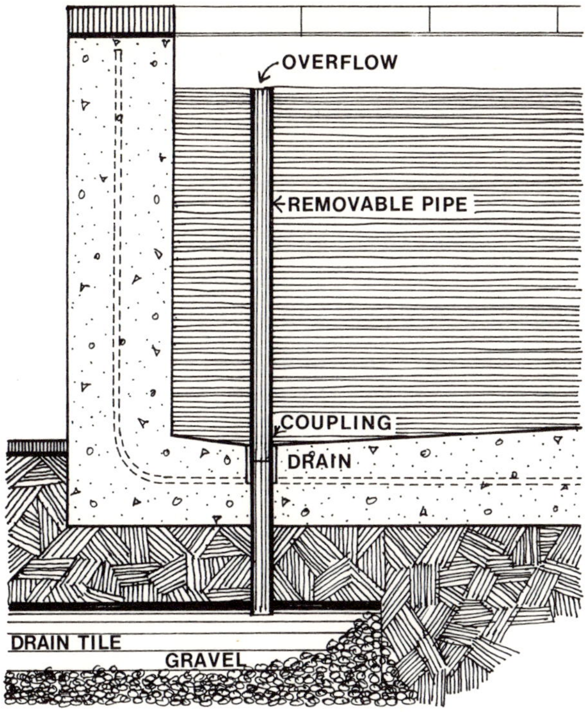

1 Combined Drain & Overflow

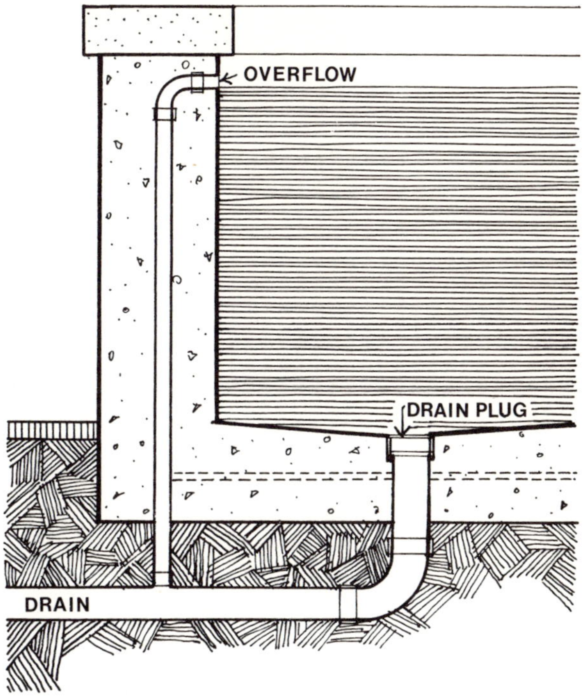

2 Separate Drain & Overflow

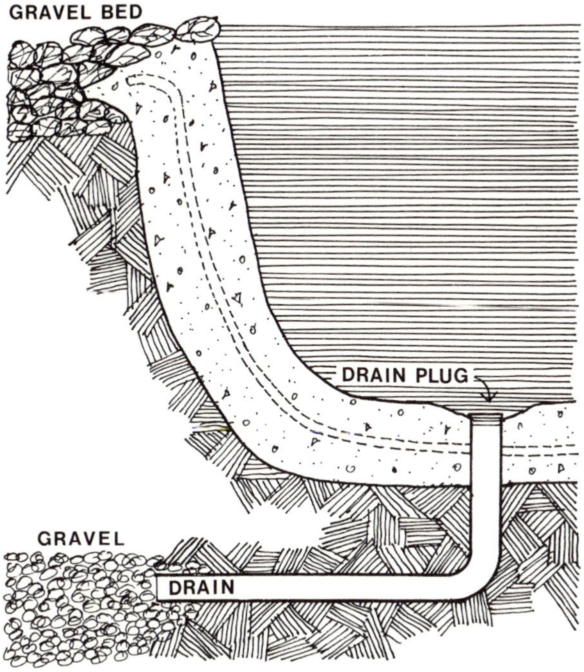

3 Ground Overflow, Separate Drain

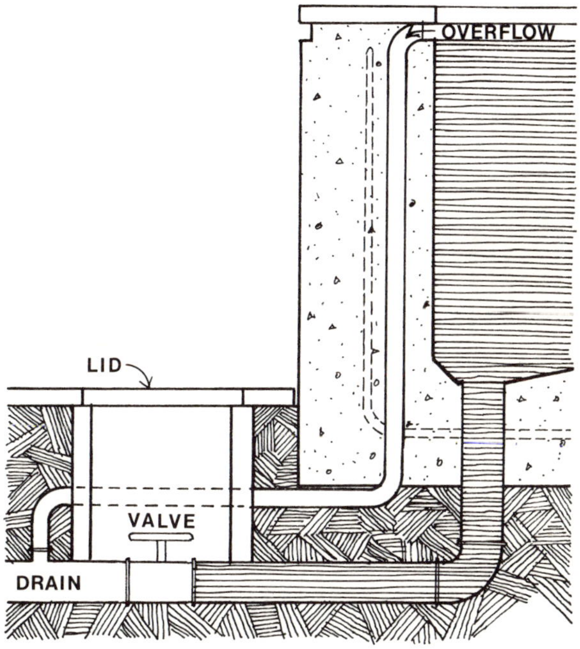

4 Drain with Shutoff Valve

DRAINAGE & OVERFLOW

ADRIÁN MARTÍNEZ

A raised pool bordered with tile; fountains and sculpture complete this handsome setting. (Architectural Pottery Co. photo)

by hand. Be sure the soakaway pit is large enough to absorb all the water. If an overflow pipe is required, install it at the same time as the drainage pipe and connect the pipes.

To change water in the pool, place a hose in the pool at a 45° angle, with a gentle flow of water. After 20 minutes turn off the water and then restart.

Overflow can be taken care of by a drywell. Dig a hole lower than the pool. Fill it with stones, run an overflow pipe from the pool to the well, and cover the well with planks and soil. Use 1.5 or 2-inch diameter galvanized pipe, and put it in place at the bottom of the pool before any concrete is poured. Cover the pipe hole with perforated zinc so that fish cannot enter. Set the coupling of brass into the floor of the pool; the coupling should be set an inch or so below the surface of the pool floor so that the surrounding area slopes to it.

Coping and Edges

The coping or edge of the pool is the frame, the finishing touch to the water garden. Some pools do not have this decorative trim, but most pools are better looking with it.

The formal traditional pool calls for coping that is formal in appearance—brick, tile, cut stone, or even concrete block. The paving may be laid in a simple pattern to match the look of the pool; put it in place in a mortar bed.

If you decide to use decorative ceramic tile for the edges of the pool you will need special grouts and cements (available from a tile dealer).

Raised Pools

A raised pool has a low wall and is constructed like a sunken pool, with one exception: both inside and outside wooden forms for walls are needed to shape the concrete shell. The walls may be a few inches or a few feet above ground level and can be capped with brick, stone, or tile.

A raised pool provides a convenient seating ledge, and, unlike a sunken pool, the wall acts as a safety precaution for children or pets.

You can also protect toddlers by setting screens on bricks or stones just a few inches below the water surface. The screen can be wire mesh, with spaces between the wires so that it will not hinder water plants. The brick or stones can be put into the walls when the pool is built. The screenwork is secured to a pipe framework which rests on pegs. The water in the pool obscures the screen from view, and fish and plants are not bothered by it.

Planting the Formal Pool

The formal pool is the feature of the garden, and the scene is elegant and impressive. Frames of greenery are not really needed; the pool alone makes the statement. However, this does not rule out some accessory plantings in containers near or in the pool. Terra cotta pipe sections with tall umbrella plants can be very effective. Elevate the tubs on bricks in the pool so that only the decorative rims of the pipes show. Or use architectural designed tubs or pots (see list of suppliers at end of book) placed at different levels in the water. Also, horsetail

Cyperus accents this brick lined pool; border boxes of various plantings help to set off the scene. (Author photo)

plants (Equisetum) or bamboo (Phyllostachys) and water iris are ideal for tubs and pots and appropriate near water.

With a raised pool, place tubs and pots at the water's ledge. Select white or beige containers; avoid bright colors that steal the show from plants and pool. Reproductions of classic urns and pots are other good choices for pool ledges or you can put them adjacent to the pool if it is not raised. Almost any plant can be grown in a container, but select species with arching and graceful branches; they are more in harmony with the water picture. (For specific plants and descriptions see Chap. 9.)

Other formal-pool decorations are concrete cylinders and blocks; they are placed in the water at different levels in a random pattern.

Brick paving and edging frame this water garden pool. (Clint Bryant photo)

Ground cover and bricks are part of a formal pool picture. (Author photo)

4. Natural or Informal Pools

The natural or informal pool or pond is very much like a rock garden; both create within themselves a distinctive picture, and in them plants and animals play a vital role. Also, both must be artificially built and a part of the total landscape.

Although the natural pool can have many names—stream, brook, lake, pond—for us it will mean a body of water that has no visible square corners or man-made edges. It does have native stone and plants so that it is an integral part of the environment—it looks natural. It is not easy to duplicate nature, and these pools require great care and much more planting than a formal pool. Rocks and plants must be carefully selected, and the site for the natural pool is extremely important. If possible, it should be seen from a distance rather than close up; it should provide a pretty picture.

The pool can be large or small, a custom-made concrete shell or a prefabricated one-piece molded pool. What you select depends upon the site and how much space is available for the pool. In a small garden, a prefabricated unit would be suitable; in a larger garden, the custom-built pool better suits the scene.

Scale also is vitally important. The pool must belong to the setting; in many cases, it becomes *the landscape.* Choose a low place in the garden, for this is where water is most often seen in nature.

Frame the water with tall plants: grasses and picturesque trees. Include vertical greenery so that there is visual balance between the pool and its setting. Putting the informal pool in place is somewhat like painting a picture; there must be design, composition and balance.

Most natural pools are free-form shells of reinforced concrete. The

This pond runs through the property; it is a concrete shell and attractively landscaped with lush perimeter plantings. (Clint Bryant photo)

edges are always hidden, either with stones, a few well-placed rocks, or a frame of plants. The shell is 4 to 6 inches thick and is poured like the floor of a formal pool.

Make the rim of the pond a gentle slope so that it will look natural and will not be shattered by strong frost. The outline of the pool should have graceful, sweeping lines; there should be nothing formal about the design. A circle or an ellipse (or variations) shape is best. Design the pool so that only the water surface is visible, and, as mentioned, the hard edges are camouflaged with plants and stones.

Building the Pool

Previously, a pool had to be made by a professional mason, but now with the new materials and methods almost anyone handy with tools can build a small cement pool. As mentioned, this pool differs from the formal kind in that it has sloping sides rather than vertical walls.

Perspective

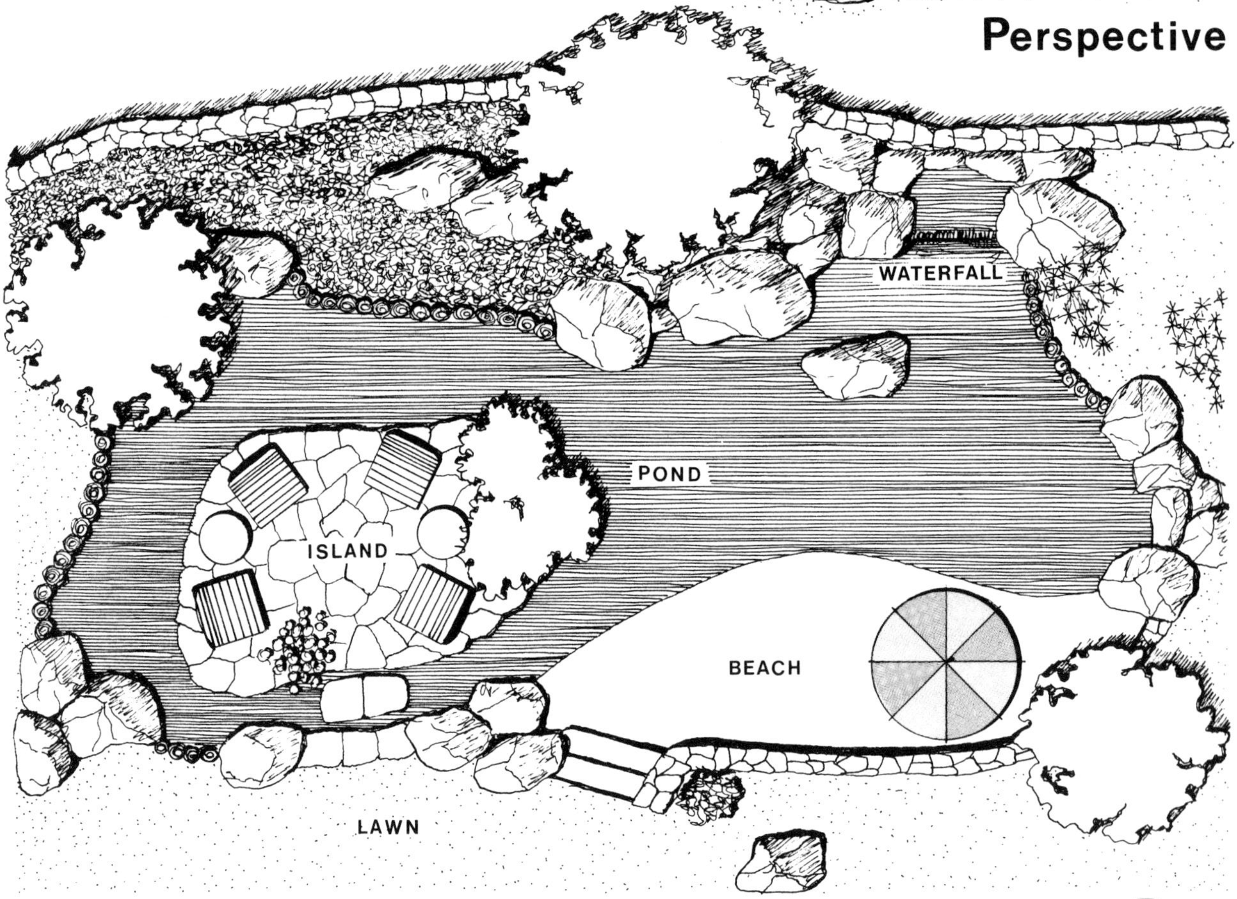

Plan

IRREGULAR POND DESIGN: ADRIÁN MARTÍNEZ

Mark out the shape of the pool on the ground with a string or a pointed tool, and work to that design. Excavate to about 2 feet, and cover the bottom of the hole with small stones to form a good solid base for the cement. The base must be absolutely firm and true to prevent the soil from sinking as this will cause cracks in the bottom of the pool. Reinforce the floor with heavy mesh wire or with rods and then use a concrete mix of 1 part cement, 2 parts sand, and 5 parts broken rubble or stone. You can mix the cement in a rented mixer or in a wheelbarrow.

Work in a 3-inch layer of concrete into the excavation over the reinforcing material; then add another 3-inch layer of concrete and smooth it with a board. If you want drain pipes, install them before any concrete is to be poured. Leave the concrete floor for a few hours and then sprinkle it lightly with water. Leave it for a few days and then sprinkle it again.

For the sides of the pool use a thinner concrete of 1 part cement to 3 parts sand, without any aggregate. Beat down the sides of the hole with a spade to get rid of loose soil, and put some plastic liner around the top edges so that loose soil will not fall into the concrete. Use rubble backfill to strengthen the face of the excavation and to act as a textured surface so that cement will adhere.

You will need to apply two layers of cement to line the sides. Make the first layer 3 inches thick, and let it dry 48 hours. Set chicken or stucco wire in place as a reinforcement; put it over the first layer of wet concrete, and spread it up the sides so that the whole shell is lined with mesh. Then apply the second 3-inch layer of concrete over the wire, and cover it thoroughly. Trowel it smooth.

Concrete must set slowly to avoid cracks and leaks. Cover it with burlap and keep the material moist for about 10 days. Before adding fish or plants the pool must be cured so that lime in the concrete does not harm wildlife.

If the pool is large you will have to install drain pipes (small pools do not need them). Construct an underground pipe outlet to a gravel-pit soakaway set to one side of the pool. In most cases, pools need emptying only once a year. Where there is a good growth of plants and the pool is stocked with goldfish and other creatures, water stays fresh a long time because the biological balance is maintained as it is in nature. (See Chap. 11).

A free-form informal pool with rocks and water lilies is partially shaded with graceful hanging trees. (Author photo)

In summer, green algae—tiny microscopic plants— may multiply in excessive sunlight and make the pool a green brew. Use a product called Argucide (available from pool suppliers), and follow directions to the letter.

If you would rather not use chemicals, make a shading device (an overhead screen) and set it over the algae for a few days; without sunlight the creatures cannot live. Of course, if there are water lilies in the pool the pads cut off much direct sunlight and algae do not multiply.

Do not use any artificial fertilizers or insecticides in the garden pool. Even a weak solution of phosphate can kill the water creatures that are essential to the ecological balance.

One-Piece Molded Pools

These are generally of irregular design and are fiberglass or plastic. The largest I have seen holds about 200 gallons of water and is approximately 8 x 6 feet in area and 18 inches deep; the smallest is about 5 feet in diameter, 7 inches deep, and holds about 50 gallons of water. One-piece molded pools are popular because they are easier to install than concrete pools and they are moderately priced.

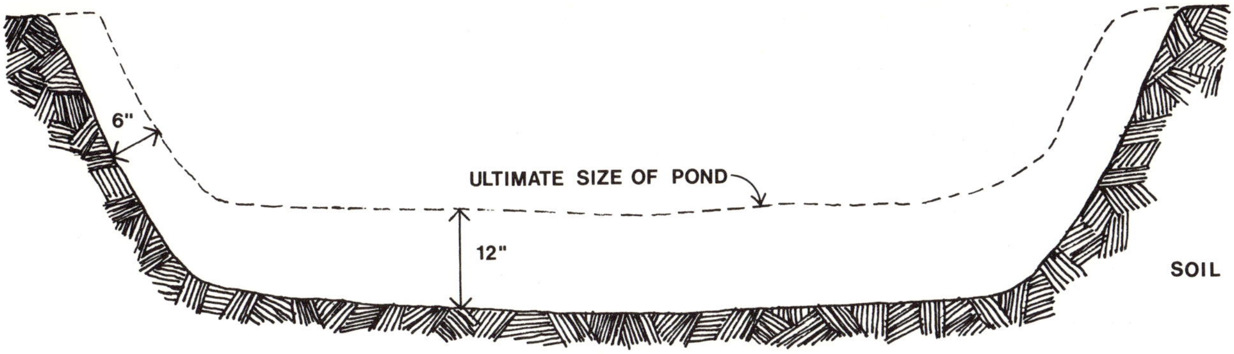

1 DIG HOLE 12" DEEPER AND 6" WIDER ON EACH SIDE THAN ULTIMATE SIZE, DAMPEN AND TAMP SOIL

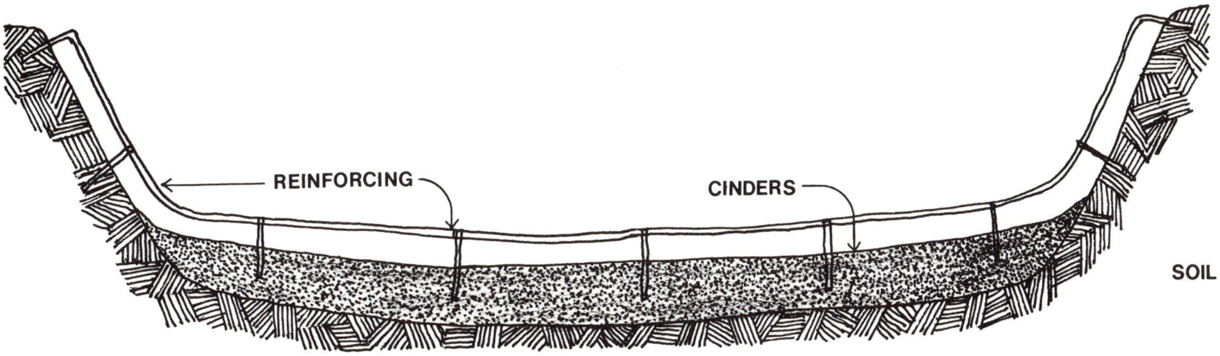

2 FILL WITH 6" OF CINDERS, SET REINFORCING 3" ABOVE ON RODS

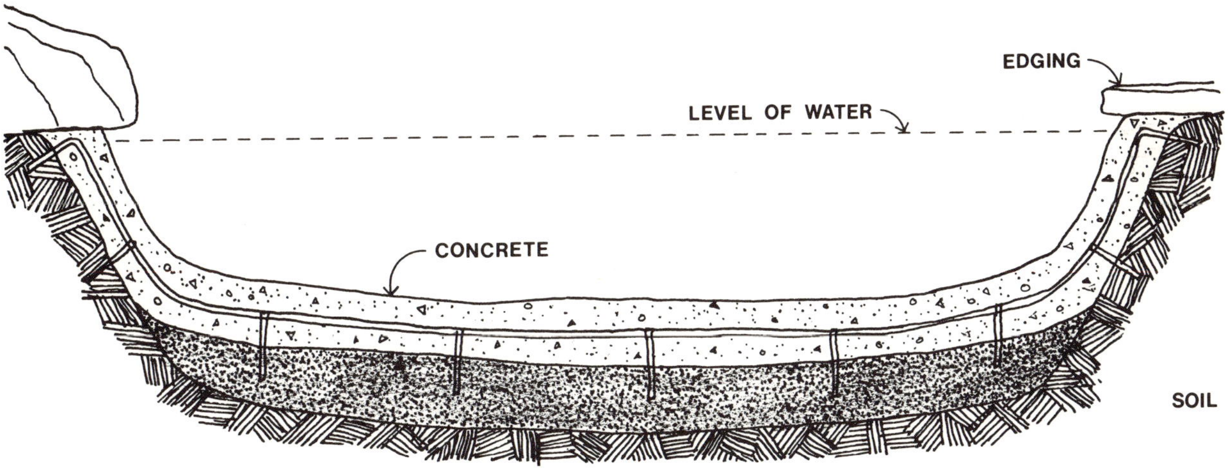

3 POUR AND TAMP CONCRETE TO 6" DEPTH, EDGE WITH STONES, ALLOW TO CURE AND FILL WITH WATER

INFORMAL POND CONSTRUCTION

ADRIÁN MARTÍNEZ

Plasto Pool Inc. offers a freeform water pool for small gardens. (Plasto Pool Inc. photo)

The small pool in my garden was installed before plastics were available but gardeners say that the new molded containers are very satisfactory. Deep digging is not necessary for their installation; the pool can be sunk to half its depth. The excavated soil is then packed around the sides. When preparing the excavation for the resin pool remove all sharp pointed stones, for in time they may penetrate the base and cause damage.

These pools should be landscaped in the same manner as concrete pools so that they appear natural. Hide edges with stones, rocks or a ground cover and frame the water with background plants.

This type of pool has no drainage or overflow apparatus. Change the water by siphoning or with a bucket.

Flexible Materials for Pools

Polyethylene or plastic liners conform to the shape of the excavation and are loosely held in place with heavy stones. Water is added to the liner gradually, the weight taking the material down until it is molded to the shape of the depression. The loose flap around the edges is concealed with stones or rocks. (Some of the liners come with a metal edging.)

For this type of pool, dig a hole about 24 inches deep and in the shape desired. Slope the sides gradually at an angle of about 30 degrees. Remove all stones from the excavation, and cover the ground with fine sand or tamped-down soil. Stretch the material to fit the depression.

Liners are a quick way to have a summer pool; however, it is doubtful that the material will last over the years.

Planting

The large custom made informal pool will need extensive planting to make it attractive. (Smaller one-piece pools do not need so much greenery.) Vertical plants provide protection from the wind, and are a desirable foil for the smaller marginal plants that accompany water lilies and other floating aquatics.

This man-made terrazzo water garden is attractive in a Chicago garden. The pool is handsomely landscaped with poolside plantings. (Eldon Danhausen photo)

At water's edge, put in some perennials and low-growing dwarf trees such as pine or spruce. Choose low, round forms so that there is a natural blending from water to plants rather than an abrupt change in height. Select a weeping willow *(Salix babylonica)* or perhaps *Robinia tortuosa.* There is also a golden Willow *(Salix vitellina*

A concrete shell was the material used for this informal pool. (Author photo)

A waterfall cascades over lush ivy plants in this informal pool scene. (Clint Bryant photo)

A fine informal pool is beautifully framed with rocks and stones. (Featherock Inc. photo)

var. *pendula)* that is handsome. Weeping birch *(Betula pendula)* is another fine choice, the graceful pendulous branches are always attractive near water.

Many poplars thrive in wet soil too, and bamboo, usually avoided by most gardeners because it grows so rampantly, is still one of my favorites. Its airy appearance and tall growth are especially handsome near the water.

In shady areas, consider azaleas and hydrangeas; they do very well at pool side. To balance the design try taller plants such as *Carex aristata.* Water spurge *(Euphorbia palustris)* is another good candidate around the pool edges and yellow skunk cabbage *(Lysichitum Americanum),* despite its name, is a beautiful plant near pools. It has giant spinach-like leaves, showy all through summer and autumn. Arrowhead *(Sagitarria sagittifolia)* is always desirable with its ornamental foliage, as is water plantain hosta and white-striped sweet flag *(Acorus calamus variegatus).*

Fit the plants in curving, sweeping lines; use height and mass to balance the landscape. However, remember that most plants in the water—lilies and lotus—will need light, so don't plant trees and shrubs that will grow too tall and obscure the sunlight. Always leave a clearing and paths to the pool so that it is easy to view the water scene.

For other planting ideas, see Chap. 9 and 10.

5. *Fountains and Cascades*

Centuries ago, the impressive fountains in Italy and Spain were elaborate works of art that formed architectural and sculptural shapes. At a great expense water was often piped in from streams miles away.

Today's fountains are much less expensive and complicated and more sophisticated than even a few years ago. New designs and materials (recirculating pumps, dishes, fiberglass, and so forth) have made it feasible for anyone to enjoy the sight and sound of water in motion.

How you use water as a decorative element in your garden—fountain, waterfall, or cascade—depends on the individual landscape and space available and your own preferences. Sometimes, the fountain may need (depending on the water pressure in your home) the addition or extension of a cold-water line. However, a recirculating pump is usually sufficient.

Types of Fountains

Reproductions of classical fountains are still available from a few suppliers, but they are expensive, and few properties have the space for them. Modern fountains although less spectacular than classical ones, are still dramatic. The jet fountainhead is a recent innovation and contains a rotary principle that produces myriad droplets, each forming a light prism. The form of the water may be a simple jet or a more elaborate tier pattern or ribbons and bubbling bouquets of water.

Rococo and Baroque figures and forms have been replaced by simple and lightweight metal or fiberglass dishes, or simply the jet itself, without any ornamentation.

A cascade arrangement using prefabricated dishes; recirculating pump is the water source. (Clint Bryant photo)

The simplest way to put water in motion is to have a single stream rising from a vertical jet; or use a brass ring with jets on the supply pipe at or below water level. The water can be controlled from a slow trickle to a height of 8 or 9 feet. The jet pipe may have a large or small opening or may be pinched or flared to produce many different water effects.

Pedestal fountains that look like bird baths and have water circulating through piped figures are also at suppliers. Some are made of fiberglass; others are stone, and include a recirculating pump. However nice these may be they cannot be considered fountains in the true sense but rather a spot of water in the garden. They are rarely impressive or elegant, and they can never substitute for the beauty of an authentic fountain. Use them carefully to avoid disappointments.

Elevation

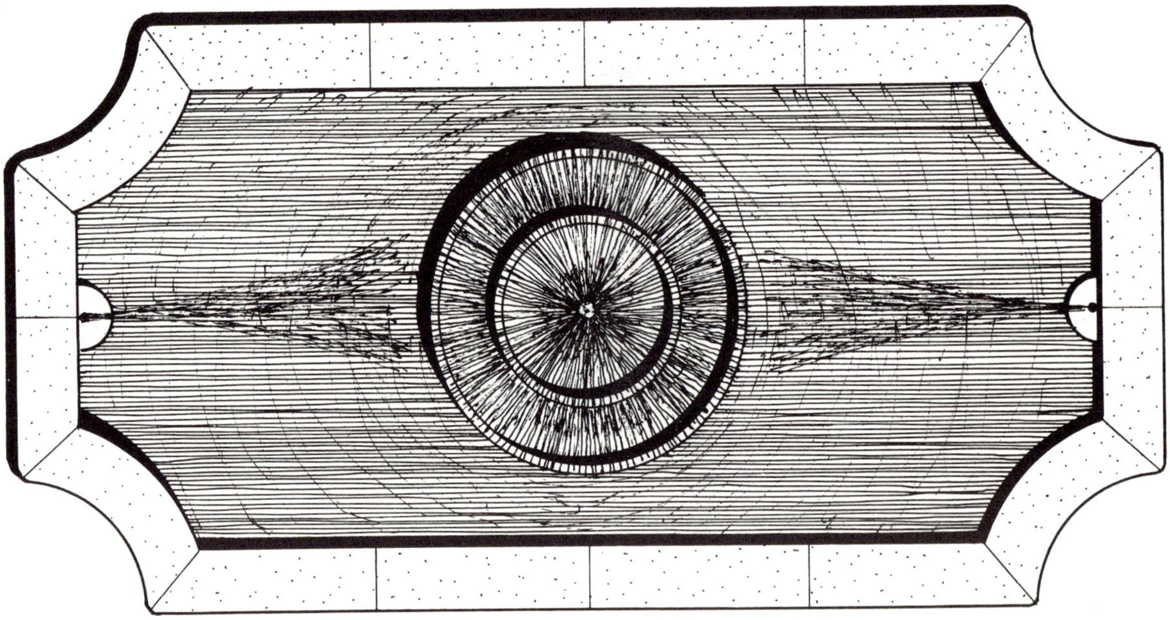

Plan

FORMAL POOL & FOUNTAIN DESIGN: ADRIÁN MARTÍNEZ

SINGLE VERTICAL JET

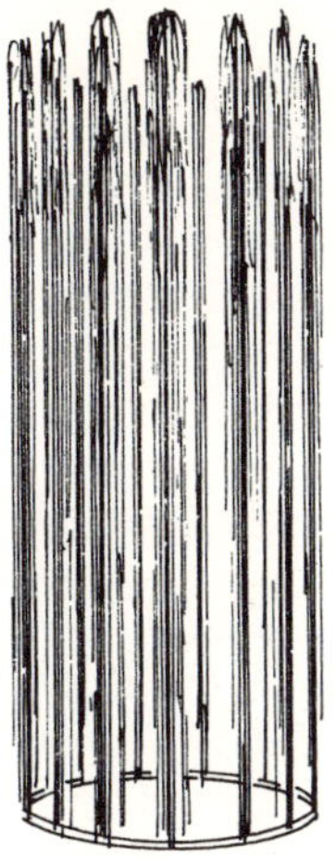

MULTIPLE VERTICAL JETS

INWARD SLANTED JETS

OUTWARD SLANTED JETS

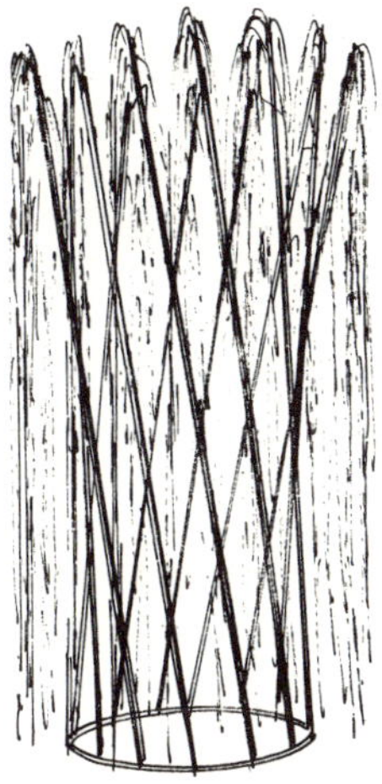

DIAGONALLY SLANTED JETS

AERATED VERTICAL JET

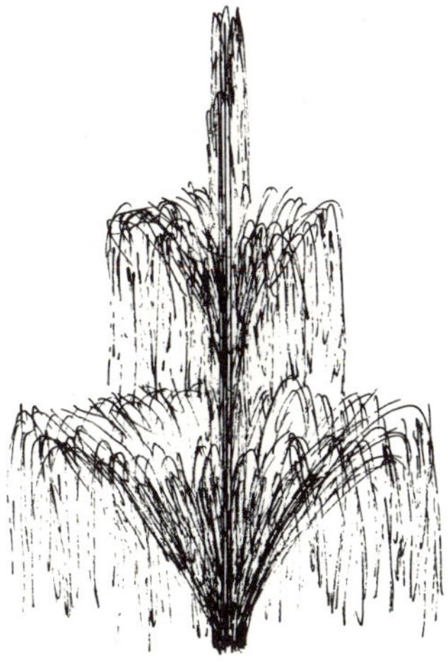

MULTIPLE TIERED JETS

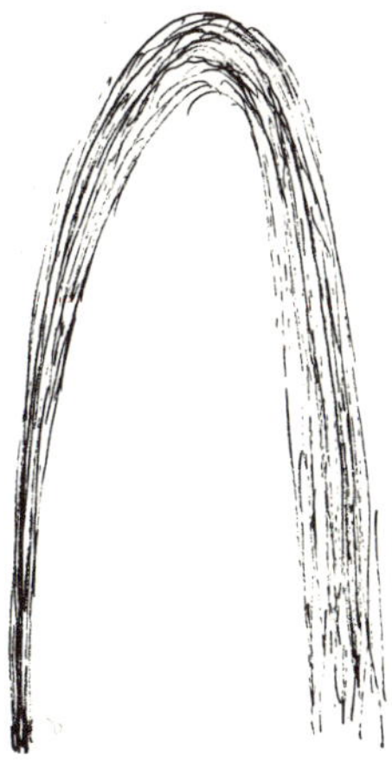

SINGLE ARCHED JET

FUNNEL SHAPED JET

FOUNTAIN JET PATTERNS

ADRIÁN MARTÍNEZ

Attractive plantings are the background for a waterfall; the informal pool is further enhanced by a carpet of green. (Clint Bryant photo)

The Fountain in the Landscape

The fountain can be bought as a separate unit and placed in an existing pool, but more often it comes with its own basin. The basin or pool for the average fountain need be only 10 inches deep. If you already have a pool with water plants you will not be able to add any type of extensive fountain because water in motion will disturb the surface of the water and the plants. Small figures for fountain edges are an exception; these are piped for water.

Do not put a fountain in an informal pond; it will be out of place and ruin the effect. The fountain, no matter how simple, has an elegant and formal appearance, and its only place in the garden is as a feature for a formal pool.

Put the fountain where it can be seen by guests and where you can see it; it should provide a pleasant picture from a house or terrace. A corner on a terrace is a good place for a fountain. It is out of the way of traffic but still easy to see. A fountain with a high spray needs some protection so that wind doesn't blow the water in all directions. A wall, hedge, or trees add beauty and background and protect water spray.

This concrete aggregate fountain is small but charming in this garden. (Brock Arms photo)

Three fountains accent a building exterior. (Architectural Pottery photo)

Fountains that disturb the water make it impossible to easily grow water lilies. However, the wall fountain that is a carved mask, piped for water, causes a minimum of disturbance in the basin. Place plants in boxes close to the edge of the pool.

Although fountains can be striking with plain backgrounds of pavings or lawns, some are equally handsome with plants around them; urns or stone vases with graceful plants are appropriate. Moving water needs some kind of power. It is possible to tie into the main drain of the property, allowing endless operation of the fountain, but it is much easier to use a recirculating pump. Or buy a fountain kit that already contains the pump that recirculates the water, and permits the growing of fish and plants, and aerates the water. (Most municipal water supplies have chemicals that kill all organisms necessary to fish and plants.) For information on pumps see Chap. 6.

A handsome small fountain, classical in design, as viewed through a pergola. The lattice doorway handsomely frames the water accent. (Photo courtesy Rosedown Gardens)

A unique wall waterfall at Longue Vue Gardens in New Orleans. (Photo courtesy Longue Vue Gardens, Jim Kennedy, photographer)

Cascades and Waterfalls

Waterfalls require great volumes of water and are lovely, but they require professional help. They are impressive installations worth the expense and may take many forms, depending on the property and your budget. See Drawing 8 for a typical waterfall system.

Cascades are a simple way to provide the sight and sound of tumbling water and are a dandy garden accent in arid climates. Basically, water falls from one object to another; the object may be a ledge, a metal pan, a rock cropping, or a series of metal bowls.

Cascade basins are available at suppliers and are made of metal, plastic, or stone, with a wide lip in front so that water can easily flow from the dish. Three are sufficient for the average garden; have a small pool at the bottom to catch the water. A small pump (similar to a fountain pump) stands on the ledge in the bottom of the pool, and plastic tubing takes the water upwards; the same water is recirculated. The operation is simple and the effect is attractive.

Instead of commercial dishes, pieces of metal or stone set into a concrete or brick wall produce a similar effect. The water may pour from each individual outcropping to form three cascades or, as with the dishes, may fall from one ledge to the next and then into the pool. There are numerous variations, and what you use depends on your imagination.

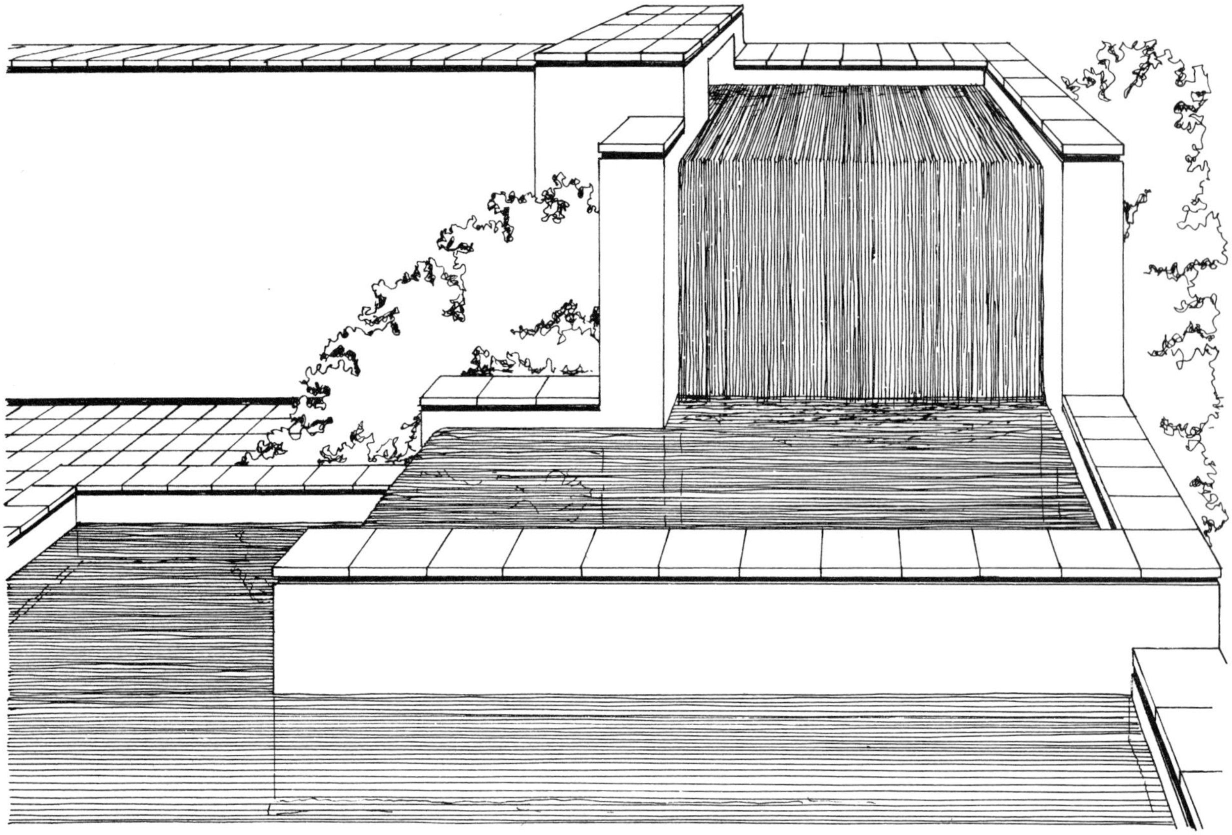

Perspective

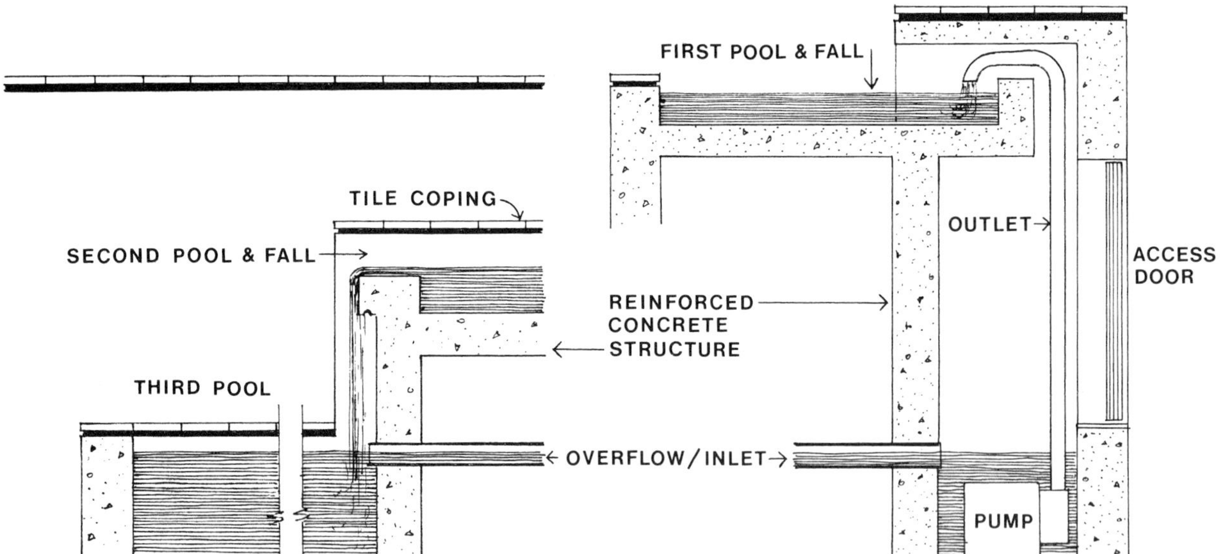

Detail

Pump Housing

WATERFALL DESIGN: ADRIÁN MARTÍNEZ

Perspective

NOTE: POOL STRUCTURE IS REINFORCED CONCRETE

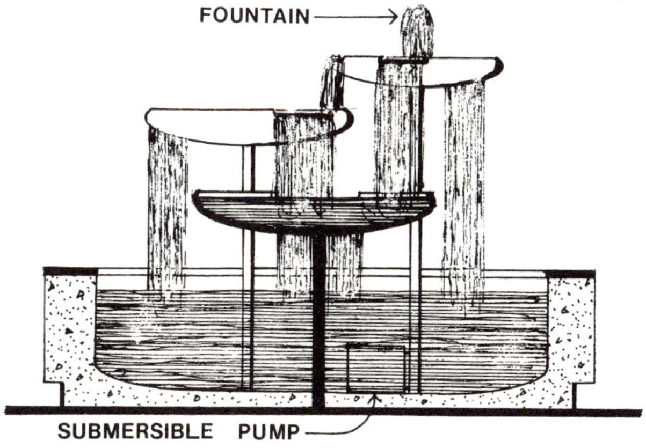

Section

Plan

DISC CASCADE

DESIGN: ADRIÁN MARTÍNEZ

This classical fountain with a single jet is at Longue Vue Gardens in New Orleans; it is similar to the fountain in the Generalife in Granada, Spain. (Photo courtesy of Longue Vue Gardens; Jim Kennedy, photographer)

With cascades, much depends on how the water strikes the surface of the objects and how far apart they are placed. Water falling from different heights can produce a soft tinkling sound, like rain on a lake, or a heavy stream plunging into the pool can sound like water running over a pebbly brook. You can create these effects by varying the placement and size of the ledges.

The main pool for a cascade should have a surface of at least 25 square feet and be roughly 5 feet square or, if circular, have a diameter of 5 feet.

Most large water lilies will not tolerate turbulent or constant water-temperature change, but there are other plants that succeed well. Small water lilies, rushes, and ferns in containers will brighten the pool area.

Be sure basins are level and solidly supported, and observe the esthetic rule and keep the cascades in harmony with the setting.

Left: *An elaborate formal pool and cascade fountain plays an important part of a garden area.* (Photo courtesy Longue Vue Gardens, Jim Kennedy, photographer)

6. Pool Mechanics and Care

Many people who want water gardens hesitate to install them because they think it is a complicated and expensive procedure. It doesn't have to be if you are willing to do some of the work yourself. And working with concrete and wooden forms, plumbing, pumps, and pipes need not be a mystery if you have a little knowledge.

Concrete

Concrete is not difficult to work with if you use a rented, half-bag mixer; you just add the materials. Generally, concrete is the most popular pool material. It has a number of advantages: it is basically strong, can be cast into almost any shape, can be reinforced easily with wire mesh or rods when necessary, is simple to finish smoothly (no paints or sealers are needed; simply run the edge of a board over it), and, because of its smooth surface, it discourages algae.

Concrete does have some disadvantages. It generally requires wooden forms for pouring (to avoid weak joints), and it is heavy.

A standard concrete formula is 1 part cement, 2 parts sand, and 3 parts aggregate. The mix should be stiff so that it pours slowly from a shovel. Sacked cement and sand is available at dealers and coarse aggregate is sold by the cubic yard. For 1 sack of cement, 2 sacks of sand, and 3.5 cubic yards of aggregate you will need about 5 gallons of water for mixing.

Sand must be free of foreign matter (including soil) or weak spots will develop in the floors or walls. Stones should be no larger than 1.5 inches in diameter. Never leave sacks of cement outdoors without protection; if it rains they will be useless.

Small amounts of concrete can be mixed with a shovel on a board, but for a large pool, mixing is best done with a half-bag power mixer. First put in the cement and sand in the drum, and let them blend for a few minutes. Add the stones, and allow the mixer to turn some more until they are coated with the cement/sand solution. Add water, about 2.5 gallons for a half sack of cement. Let the mixer turn for about 3 minutes or until the cement, sand, and stones are thoroughly blended; then it is ready to be poured for walls or floors. Tip the drum, and pour the concrete into a wheelbarrow.

Pumps and Fountains

Overflow and drainage have been discussed and illustrated previously (Chap. 3). Electrical fountain pumps were mentioned in the preceding chapter, but since there are so many of them in so many sizes some further information is given here. These notes should provide enough preliminary information so that you can talk intelligently when purchasing the right pump for the job. Electrical installations always should be approved by local codes and installed by qualified people.

Pumps for pool fountains are generally of two types: surface pumps in which the unit is outside the pool and the submersible pump where the unit is underwater. The pump is a complex of whirling blades; water passes over the blades and is pressured into further motion; the same water is recirculated. Fish and plants can be grown in this water in contrast to an everchanging supply of tap water that contains chemicals detrimental to wildlife.

Fully submersible pumps (the motors are in sealed domes) operate silently. They are placed in the floor of the pool, and tubing carries water to the fountain. They need no pump chamber or external piping and never require priming. There are large models with an output of 25 gallons/minute at a head of 30 feet, and smaller pumps with a capacity of 5 gallons/minute that can throw a $\frac{5}{16}$-inch water jet to about 4 feet. The pump has a waterproof cable sealed into the dome; the cable is led along the pool bottom and over the side to a waterproof connector. Another cable leads to outlets on the house. Put pumps on small bricks or stone platforms at the bottom of the pool to allow the jet to stand just above the water.

Other pumps (non-submersible) are available in horizontal or

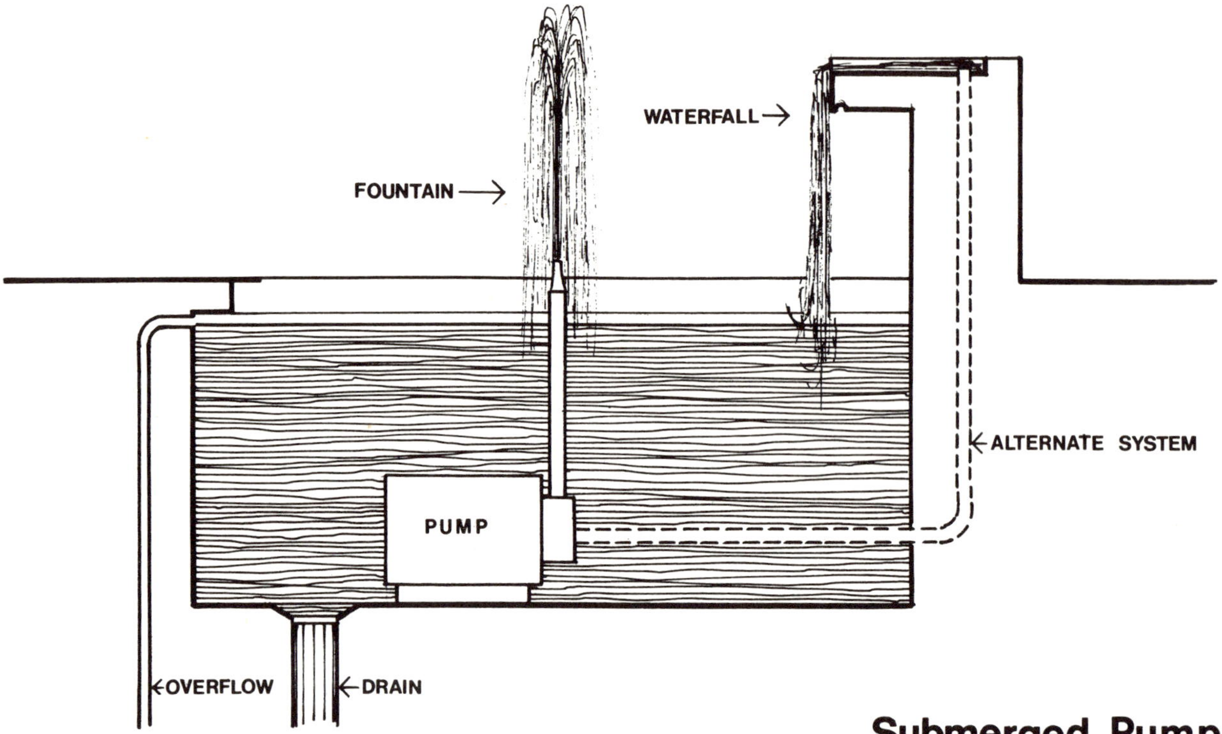

Submerged Pump

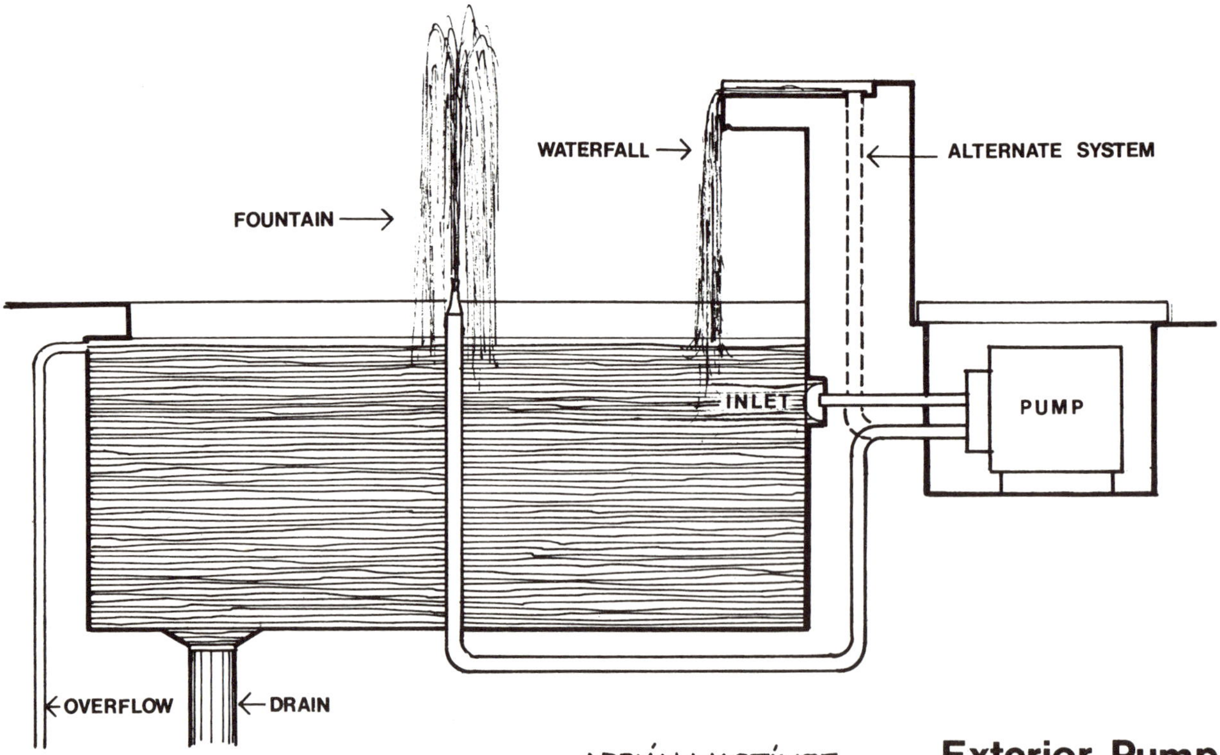

ADRIÁN MARTÍNEZ

Exterior Pump

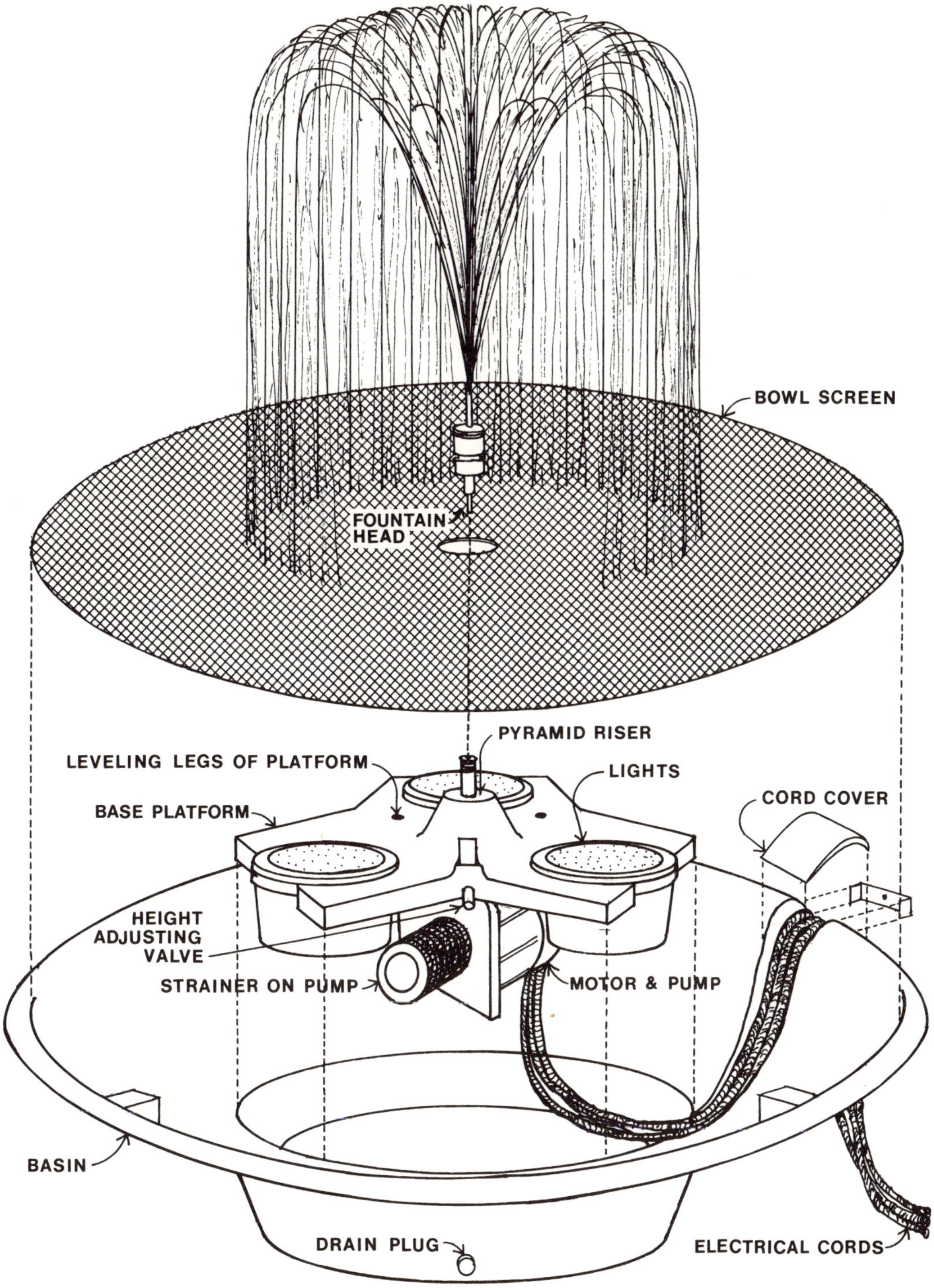

FOUNTAIN & BOWL ASSEMBLY
COURTESY OF RAIN JET CORPORATION

ADRIÁN MARTÍNEZ

Concrete is the material used for this pool shell; note the sloping edges. (Author photo)

vertical models. The horizontal pump takes the water up along a level pipe from the pool to the pump and then pushes it upwards; the vertical unit takes up the water directly and keeps it going in the same direction. The vertical pump must be in shallow water and usually requires a special compartment. The horizontal pump is installed outside the pool. These pumps are available in many sizes.

Some pumps are self priming; others need to be installed in a flooded position to retain their prime. Follow the manufacturer's directions carefully before installing and starting pumps.

The one-fiftieth horsepower motor needs about 15 watts of electricity; the one-third horsepower unit uses about 270 watts. The pump itself usually can be added to the present house lighting system without worry of overloading.

Some fountain kits come with pumps in the fountain unit itself.

Repairs and Remedies

Even with good workmanship pools can develop leaks and cracks. If the cracks are hairline there is little repairing problem: use a coat or two of special pool sealer or caulking compound. Epoxies are also available for hairline concrete cracks, or use a loose mixture of 1 part cement to 3 parts sand.

Large cracks in the walls or floors require more serious work. They are usually caused by uneven settling of the pool (if it has been poured on soft or filled ground) or by ice pressure in the winter. If you notice a crack, get at the fault immediately; if it gets too bad, nothing will repair it.

A major crack will be deep and wide and must be carefully patched. Drain the pool, then chisel away the crack to a V shape and fill it with a caulking compound forced into place with a trowel or knife. The crack can also be repaired by using a mixture of half cement and half sand; wet it only enough to make it workable. Fill the patch, smooth it over, and let dry thoroughly.

Remember that after repairing pool walls or floors, the pool must be cured again before fish or plants are added.

Pool Water

It is wise to change the pool water every spring. This will seem like undue work, for many people argue that a well-balanced pool can go for years without changing. Yet a yearly cleaning is the easiest way to avoid possible trouble. It gives you a chance to inspect the pool and to catch small hairline cracks before they become big ones. Cleaning the pool every year also eliminates the really hard scrubbing of walls and floors that is needed if the renovation is done only every fifth year.

Most pool water is never as clear as swimming-pool water. It should have a slightly green cast; this is natural and means that the balances of life in the pool—fish, algae, plants—are working together. If the water becomes thick and turgid and has a faint, unpleasant smell it indicates that trouble is brewing or has already started. In such cases the bottom of the pool will usually yield an accumulation of decomposing leaves, dead fish and snails, or other debris. (This condition is more likely to occur in the summer, when decomposition is hastened by warmth.)

If the water is sour the pool must be emptied of plants and fish and drained. Scrub the walls and floors with a solution of potassium permangenate and thoroughly hose it out several times. (When you

Water for this small pool-fountain is powered by a hidden recirculating pump. (Clint Bryant photo)

refill the pool, the water may appear purple from the solution, but it will clear up in a few days.) Use the potassium solution with care; too much will do more harm than good.

You may think that a pool will attract an undue amount of mosquitoes, but this rarely happens. Other insects find them a delight to dine on, and if there are fish in the pool, they will consume the larvae in quantity.

Winter Care

In all-year temperate climates and in mild-winter areas it is not necessary to drain pools in the winter. But in severe winters, pools should be drained before freezing weather comes. It is a good idea to put a few sticks or boards in the bottom of the pool to absorb the thrust of ice which may form after the snow has melted.

A pool also may be prepared for the winter by leaving the water level a little below normal and placing a floating log in the water. It will absorb the thrust of the ice and take the pressure off the concrete walls so that cracks cannot develop.

In areas with mild winters, water can be left in a pool if it is over a depth of 20 inches. It will freeze over, and plants and fish will hibernate through the winter. However, break the ice every few days; drill a few holes about 1 inch in diameter, and draw off a few inches of water. The holes will let oxygen enter the water and allow for the escape of toxic gases. Snow will have to be swept from the pool surface daily because light must penetrate to the plants below.

There are also small electrical immersion heaters that can be placed in pools to keep the water from freezing in the winter. They also prevent the walls from cracking from ice pressure. These heaters are available at suppliers, and one will provide enough heat for a small pool; for larger ones, two or three heaters may be necessary.

Pool Filters

These are new devices that provide a natural biological environment for your pool. The action of the filter unit destroys waste matter and excess food so that it does not stagnate at the bottom of the pool. The units are made of molded styron plastic, are non-toxic to fish and plants, and last for years. They come in three sizes. Fill the filter box with pea-sized gravel and attach the unit with vinyl plastic tubing to any submersible pump.

The walls of this formal pool are concrete, poured in wooden forms. (Author photo)

7. *Sculpture for the Pool*

Sculpture is a desirable part of the water pool. Fountains and pools of centuries past were always adorned with figures or other ornamentation, for they provided contrast and interest to the water scene.

Figures and Ornamentation

A figure or decorative piece can be used as a central motif or placed at one side of the water. There is an array of statuary, from small animals and frogs to large figures. Some are made of lead, others of bronze or stone.

Sculpture is rarely inexpensive, but since it will be a long-lasting, permanent decoration it is worth the cost. It should always be distinctive, so avoid cheap imitations, plastic gnomes, and cute figures; they do not belong near the pool.

The metal or stone adornment should fit the setting; it may be upright and horizontal, massive, or light or dark in color. Pool statuary is piped so that water is dispensed in a spray or poured from a cup, vase, or shell.

The piece must be in scale with the surroundings and should have a suitable background. For example, if you choose a tall figure, provide a suitable background: a fence or a row of shrubbery. With smaller statuary, background is less important, but with all pieces placement is vital. The statue should appear as though it belongs to the pool.

A large figure is heavy, so have ample help to put it in place. It must have a proper pedestal, and in winter must be protected from high winds that could knock it over. Some pieces are reproductions

A small cherub and an urn accents this handsome brick lined pool. (Roche photo)

of classical figures; others are cheap imitations of cupids and the like and are best left out of the garden pool. Sea shells and tiered designs, frogs, and other creatures of water origin are available. Some can be ordered separately for an existing pool; others come as a complete unit with the basin.

Beware of the plastic or imitation stone basins and dishes with figures attached. They look like bird baths and are rarely handsome in the garden.

Recently, abstract sculpture has appeared in the pool; metal pieces in various designs are very suitable for even the most formal pool. But again, they must fit the garden and house. Concrete cylinders and

An iron lantern and a whimsical frog are part of this handsome water scene. (Clint Bryant photo)

Top left: *Here concrete cylinders act as statuary in a concrete block formal pool.* (Architectural Pottery photo)

Bottom left: *Contemporary sculpture accents a pool; the hard clean lines are a good complement to the water picture.* (Architectural Pottery Co. photo)

A piped dolphin is part of a formal pool; the plantings make an ideal background for it. (Author photo)

stone blocks are also available, and even though they may not be classed as statuary they can be most handsome in the water.

If the sculpture is large it should be illuminated at night to be fully appreciated. Light it from above so that it appears natural. Place fixtures on trees or buildings near the statue. Try to position the lights so that the beams strike the statue from at least two sides. This creates a full effect of depth and three-dimensional character. Use spot or floodlights, depending on the size of the piece.

Wall Fountains

Wall fountains are less expensive than figures, and they are a good way to introduce water into the garden. They have an old-world charm that makes them very appealing. Any garden wall is immeasurably enhanced with a wall fountain. The basin can be quite shallow, for most pieces are small. The mask motif is the most popular: lion's head, frogs, or dolphins with water spouting from the face into the basin.

An informal pool is highlighted with rocks and an abstract sculpture. (Architectural Pottery photo)

If there is a wall in the garden (3 or 4 feet high), by all means consider the wall fountain. A small recirculating pump carries the water upward to the mask, and the complete installation can be made in a day.

Bronze, although expensive, is by far the best material for outdoor pieces. It is indestructible and soon develops beautiful green patina. Stone is also acceptable, although somewhat harsh; still, it offers good contrast to a wall. Cast lead is always rich in appearance and like bronze lasts a lifetime.

The dolphin fountain at Longue Vue Gardens was rendered in marble in Seville, Spain. (Photo courtesy Longue Vue Gardens; Jim Kennedy photographer)

This stature of Pan was sculptured by Josephine Knoblock of England; it decorates a unique trough fountain. (Photo courtesy Longue Vue Gardens; Jim Kennedy, photographer)

8. Nighttime Beauty With Water and Lights

Incredible beauty results when you combine water and light. Fountains sparkle with brilliance, and pools become silvery surfaces when ripples and shadows create an everchanging picture. Soft lighting and the gentle sound of water in motion are lovely to look at and offer a relaxing atmosphere.

Fountain Lighting

Underwater fountain lighting was once very tricky but not now. Most fountain kits include light fixtures—two, three, four, or five—within the unit itself. Electrical cords are furnished and a copper or bronze conduit 1.5 inches or larger must be run from the bottom of the pool to the outside. Bring the conduit up above the water level so that cords from the pump motor and lights may be carried to an outside junction box.

Lamps are generally sealed beams, and there is a choice of wattage and color lens. Light is directed up at the fountain, giving each water drop a diamond brilliance. How many lights you use and the wattage of the lamps depends upon the type of the fountain pattern you have selected. There are infinite design possibilities.

All electrical wiring for underwater lights should be in conduit as specified by the city ordinance code. Have an electrician make the conduit and wiring installation. He can then check the number of circuits necessary to operate the lights (and pump).

All electrical wiring to the fountain should be 115-volt, 60-cycle ac

A canopy light fixture adjacent to the pool illuminates water and plants.

Low voltage lighting accents the flower bed and pool and statue to make a dramatic picture. (General Electric photo)

current. Lights come with heavy-duty, three-wire cord, including a ground wire, and should be installed by an electrician before the fountain is put into operation.

There are several other types of fountain lighting: submersible low-voltage lamps that produce a very clear, sharp light; fixtures for the base of the pool aimed at the fountain; or, if there is something to attach it to, fixtures over the fountain itself (in a tree or on a fence).

Underwater light should be at the base of the fountain and aimed upward; use 15 or 25 watts of light/foot of jet height. For spray fountains aim the lighting slightly below the nozzle angle to illuminate the entire spray. Use 4 watts for each square foot of area.

Pool Lighting

There are three ways to light a decorative pool: light the water itself, light the plantings around the pool, or light both areas. Floodlights can be used to illuminate a pool, but they must be shielded and louvered types placed high in a tree or against a house wall. Avoid glare, and try to cast just an arc or soft light on the pool to simulate a moonlight effect.

Lily-pad, plastic, and low-voltage light fixtures are fine for surface lighting of water; they conceal the bulb; 2 to 4 watts of power for each square foot of water are recommended. The light is soft and subdued but bright enough to mirror the pool.

Canopy light fixtures placed in the ground around the pool are fine for balancing the pool lights. Low-voltage lights can be placed in strategic places along the pool edges. (The idea is to create a flow of light rather than concentrations of light in separate areas.)

If there are children or pets in the area it is wise to use lights at the edges of the pool for safety.

A large selection of handsomely designed light fixtures are available at suppliers. (See listing at end of book.)

A small fountain framed with trees and dramatically lighted. (Bill Locklin photo)

Low-Voltage Light Systems

These systems operate on only 12 volts and offer an inexpensive, fast way to light pools and fountains. The secret is a transformer that attaches to the side of the house and plugs into any outdoor outlet. The transformer reduces the normal 120-volt house current to 12 volts and eliminates the danger of shock even if you touch the bare wires of the cables. Unlike the normal 120-volt system the cables do not have to be buried to a great depth or enclosed in a conduit. Merely wedge the earth apart, put the cables in place in the trench, and tamp down the soil with your shoe.

Fountains lighted at night are always impressive additions to the garden. (Rain Jet photo)

Lighted, this round pool is as handsome by night as it is during the day: overhead light illuminates the pool. (General Electric photo)

Most low-voltage systems are kits with a transformer, with six to eight fixtures and about 100 feet of cable. Most kits have a resealing cable so that you can clip the fixtures to the line at any point.

Low-voltage light is soft and subdued and highly desirable for illuminating pools. Fixtures can be put around or at the base of the pool, on the water in the guise of lily pads or frogs, or under the water. For underwater installation have an electrician do the job; running wire in water is a tricky business.

If you would rather not have light around the pool, put fixtures in trees or on house eaves, and direct them at the pool to achieve a lovely moonlight effect.

9. Plants for Pool and Poolside

When we start to plan our water gardens, we immediately think of water lilies. However, there are many other beautiful plants: iris and grasses for the water edge, and floating aquatics such as water hawthorn and duckweed for the water.

Ferns with lush green fronds are attractive, too, and especially suitable near water; their graceful growth and emerald colors always command attention. They require little care and thrive in shady margins of the pool.

Native orchids and some of the pitcher-plants are unusual and tempting. However, beautiful though they may be, I have tried them several times but have never been successful with them. But my failures may be your successes so if you are fond of these lovely flowers, by all means, try some. (A list follows later in this chapter.)

Any pool is enhanced by the addition of some plants. Just what you decide to grow depends on your individual site and the kind of pool you have. The informal pool must have some greenery to make it appear natural and the formal pool too can be decorated with a few container plants. Bright foliage and colorful flowers are an integral part of the water picture.

Plants Around the Pool

These are the marsh and bog plants and include some beautiful species; perhaps you have tried some before you put in your pool and they did not succeed. Now with moist conditions they will thrive. The plants cover the demarcation between the pool and the soil and at the same time, provide a handsome setting for water lilies.

Border plants will grow in any good heavy loam and need little attention. Putting them in place at their proper planting level is important. Some like their root crowns just slightly above water level; others must have roots in marshy soil. Several need 6 to 10 inches of water above the crown of the plant.

While these are called marginal plants, most of them can be used in planting boxes, too, in the pool where they are especially handsome as bright spots of color and at the same time furnish vertical accent.

Here we include some of the more common plants for marginal plantings around the pool:

Arrowhead (Sagittaria). This is perhaps the most popular poolside plant. The dark green leaves are bold and beautiful, and the white flowers have dainty yellow centers. Plants grow to 4 feet in height and are spread by runners. Thin them occasionally if they get rampant. They grow in wet soil or in water to 6 inches in depth. Common arrowhead *(S. latifolia)*, giant arrowhead *(S. sagittifolia)*, and Japanese arrowhead *(S. japonica florepleno)* are all highly recommended.

Bulrush (Scirpus). Grasslike leaves and small spikes of flowers. Grow in bog mud or under an inch or so of water; spread rapidly but can be kept in bounds by cutting. *S. cernus* grows to about a foot and has small yellowish-white flowers. *S. lacustris* is more impressive, with dark green rushes to 9 feet and brown blooms at the tips of the stems.

Cat-tail *(Typha latifolia)*. A common bog plant that grows to 6 feet, with dark brown tails. Needs about 6 inches of water and reproduces by creeping root stock. Put in a container to confine growth. *T. latifolia* is the common cat-tail. Graceful cat-tail *T. angustifolia* is shorter, with narrow leaves and graceful tails, and pygmy cat-tail *T. minima* only grows to 12 inches.

Egyptian paper plant *(Cyperus papyrus)*. A graceful member of the sedge family. It bears fronds of thready umbrella-like leaflets at the ends of bending stems. Can grow to 10 feet. Place under 2 to 3 inches of water and in sun. *C. alternifolius* is also desirable.

Horsetail *(Equisetum hyemale)*. One of the most popular pool plants and really a beauty with its tall segmented leaves of apple green. Lovely vertical accent, and can be controlled in a container. Likes about 1 to 4 inches of water.

Taro or elephant ears *(Colocasia esculenta)*. Tuberous herbs that can reach 3 feet, with magnificent foliage shaped like elephants' ears. Put plant with root crown at water level. Needs a shady place and is a capable performer for poolside. Green taro *(C. indica)* grows to 2 feet; imperial taro *(C. antiquorum illustris)* has splotched foliage to 4 feet. Violet-stemmed taro is *C. violacea.*

Water arum *(Calla palustris)*. Grows to 12 inches, with roots in mud slightly above or below water level. Takes a while to become established, and produces white flowers in second year. Not outstanding but desirable.

Water canna (Thalia). A perennial herb similar to canna but with bold, spear-shaped foliage and deep purple flowers on long arching stems. Flourishes in an inch or so of water. *T. dealbata* grows to 4 feet, and if left on pool floor below freezing line will survive winter. *T. divaricata* is a larger form.

Sweet flag *(Acorus calamus)*. A hardy marsh perennial that likes shallow water. Has broad, dark green leaves to 3 feet. A small greenish flower is borne on a tall spike. Charming decoration for poolside.

Plantain-lily *(Hosta plantaginea)*. Desirable large, heart-shaped leaves and scented white flowers. Excellent greenery for shallow edges of pools. Spreads rapidly.

Marsh-marigold *(Caltha palustris)*. Sometimes called buttercup. A low-growing pond plant with notched leaves and lovely waxy yellow blooms in March or April. Needs root crown barely under water.

Iris. A large family, with many beardless irises that grow well in heavy moist soil or under 1 to 2 inches of water at the crowns. The appealing flowers start early in May and are bright accents near the water. *I. versicolor* is the popular and exquisite blue species. *I. kaempferi*, the Japanese iris, bears brilliant purple flowers and is not to be missed. *I. laevigata* is also handsome and similar to *I. kaempferi. I. sibirica* is tall, to 4 feet and also has blue-purple blooms. All need some sun.

Gunnera chilensis. A very large waterside foliage plant with exquisite leaves. Needs rich and loamy wet soil; crowns of plants must be above water and dry in winter. Not hardy in the North. Very similar and equally handsome is *G. manicata.*

Water plantain *(Alisma plantago)*. Almond-shaped, bright green leaves that float on water; flower stalks rise 3 feet above water.

Water lilies and Arrowheads decorate this water scene. Water plantain is in bloom in center. (Clint Bryant photo)

Azure pickerel plant *(Pontederia paniculata)*. Heart-shaped leaves and lovely blue flowers in spikes. Plants need about 12 inches of water.

New Zealand flax *(Phormium tenax)*. Broad, stiff, leathery leaves that make a bold vertical accent near the pool. Some varieties have reddish leaves, others yellow or variegated.

Babys tears *(Helxine soleirolii)*. One of the nicest creeping plants for around the pool. Grows with little care in a shady place. Don't step on it; plant it where there is no foot traffic.

Chinese water chestnut *(Eleocharis tuberosa)*. Do not confuse this plant with the true water chestnut *(Trapa natans)*. The Chinese water chestnut is a member of the Sedges. It has rush-like leaves and prefers to grow in a few inches of water.

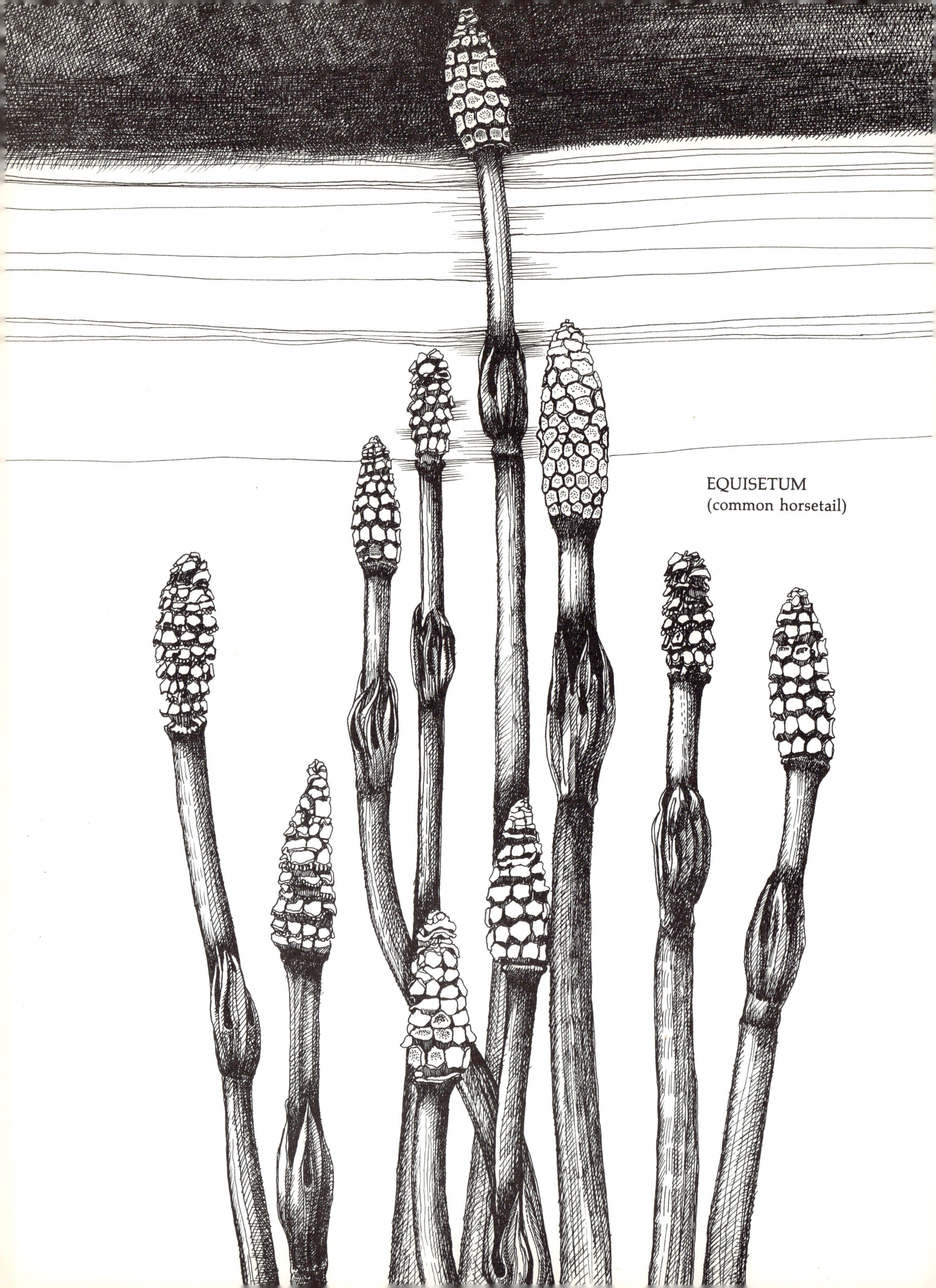

EQUISETUM
(common horsetail)

SAGITTARIA
(Arrowhead)

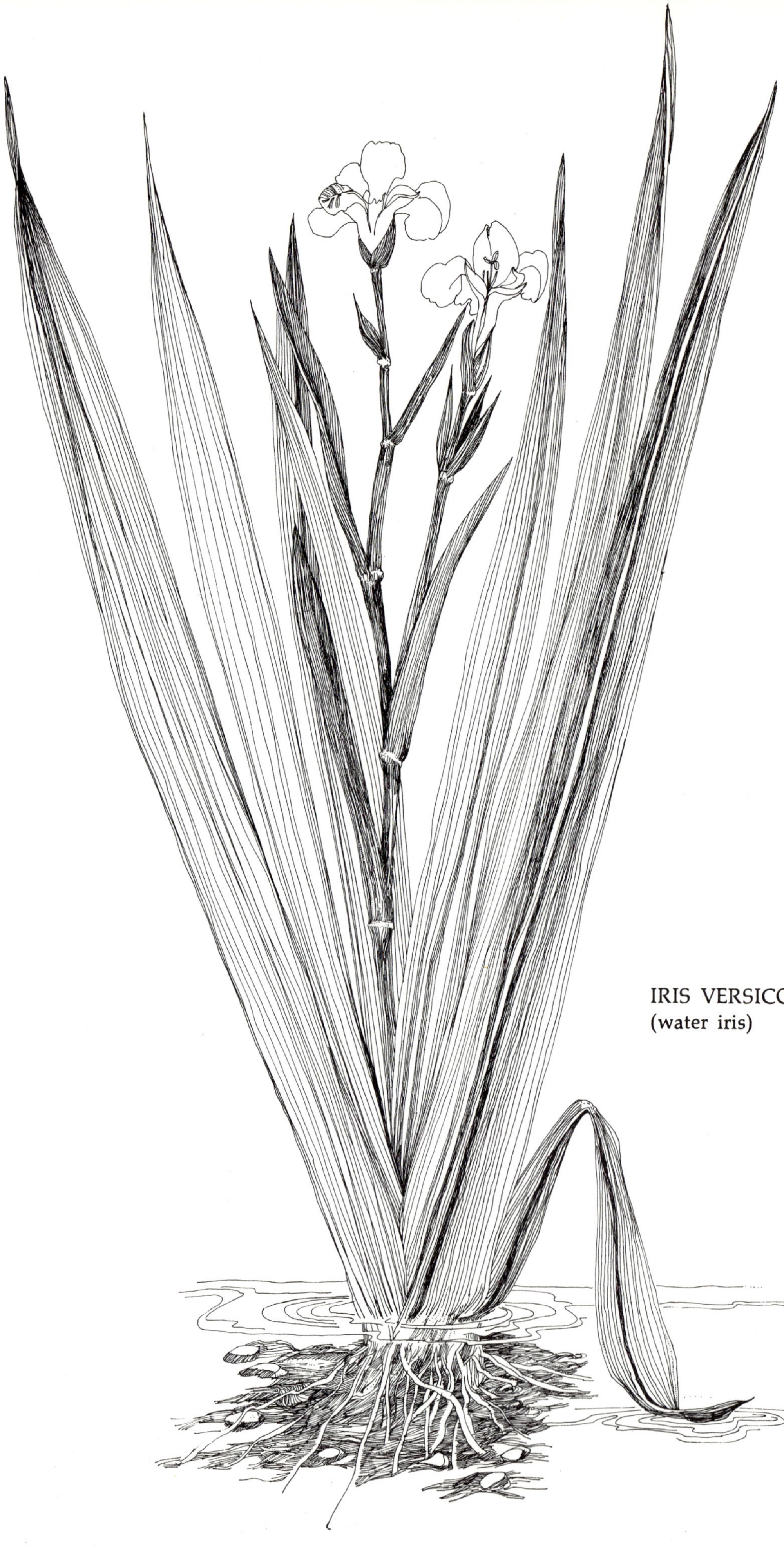

IRIS VERSICOLOR
(water iris)

LYSICHTUM AMERICANUM
(yellow skunk cabbage)

CYPERUS
(umbrella palm)

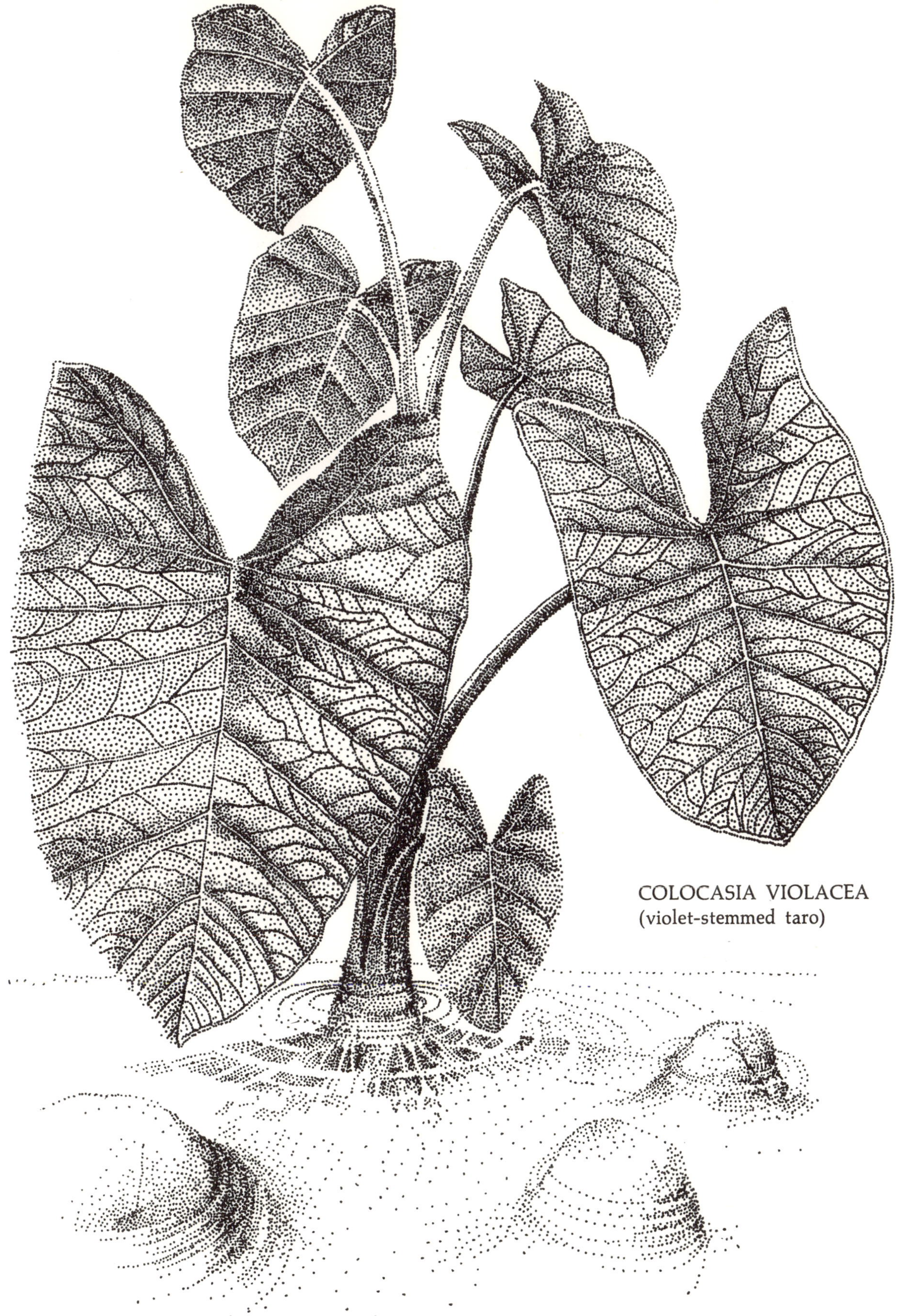

COLOCASIA VIOLACEA
(violet-stemmed taro)

CALLA PALUSTRIS
(water arum)

THALIA DEALBATA
(water canna)

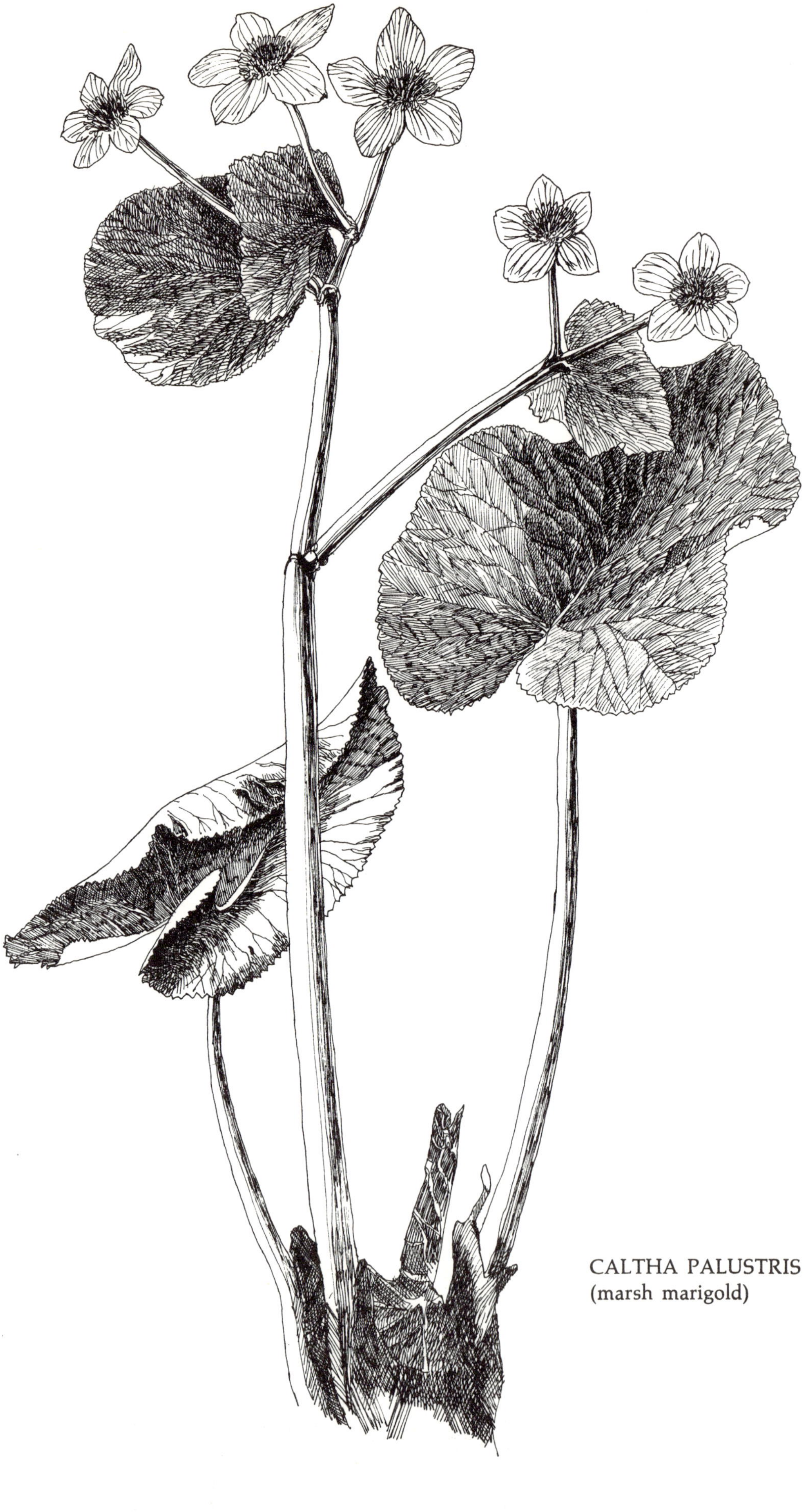

CALTHA PALUSTRIS
(marsh marigold)

ALISMA PLANTAGO
(water plantain)

PONTEDERIS PANICULATA
(azure pickerel)

EICHORNIA CRASSIPES
(hyacinth)

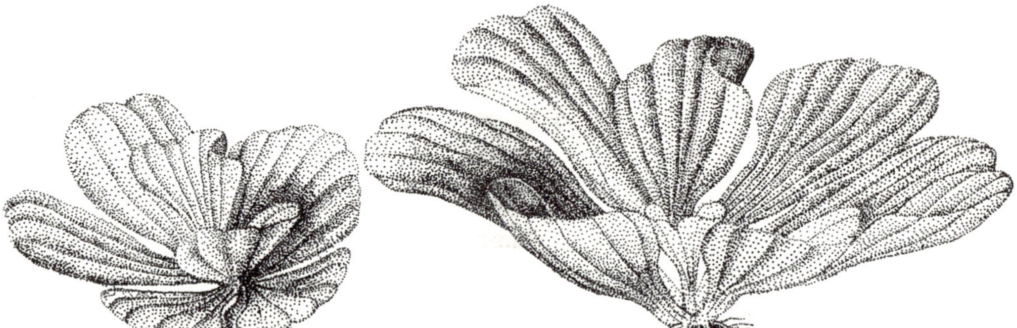

PISTIA STRATIODES
(water lettuce)

Lovely emerald ferns are the background of this attractive pool. (Clint Bryant photo)

Ferns

Ferns are always welcome near water; they are an ideal association for the informal pond or pool. Ferns, with their finely divided leaves, and Iris, with sword-shaped and erect foliage, are ideal companions.

Near water where their roots have a deep moist soil, Ferns will tolerate some sunlight and still thrive, although ideally they appreciate a shady place. The hard fern *(Blechnum spicant)* has tough dark green fronds and is a robust performer. It is evergreen and a somewhat large plant that will thrive in deepest shade. The hardy maidenhair fern *(Adiantum pedatum)* is another reliable performer, with delicate, airy, green fronds on black stems. It never grows too large.

The hart's-tongue fern *(Phyllitis scolopendium)* is always welcome near the pool, although it needs a somewhat sandy soil. The strap-shaped, deep green fronds are bold and colorful; many varieties are available and most are always lush in appearance near the water.

The marsh fern *(Dryopteris thelypteris)* produces fresh, lacy green leaves in early May; it thrives in wetness.

Osmunda cinnamonea (cinnamon fern) grows to 4 feet, a lovely tower of green, and *O. regalis* (royal fern) has pale green, almost yellow foliage. Both thrive in wet soil and some sun.

Native Orchids

These delightful plants prefer a shady position and most of them need a somewhat boggy soil. They are available from suppliers (please don't pick them from the woodlands). Buy several of them for the mortality rate is high and it seems that very few survive transplanting. Still, because they are so beautiful, they are worth the time and effort.

Calopogon. A good group of hardy orchids that thrive in wetness. *C. pulchellus* has 1 inch pink-and-yellow flowers and will need some sun. *C. borealis* has pink blooms and succeeds in shade.

Cypripedium. The popular lady-slipper orchids with many showy species. *C. acaule* bears a large solitary pink-purple flower and likes a

These water plants have been put into planting boxes, visible through the water. Plants are water cannas. (Author photo)

Chinese water chestnut, a plant that belongs to the Sedge family, graces this poolside with rush-like leaves. (Clint Bryant photo)

moist place. *C. pubescens* is yellow and delights in wet soil. *C. spectabilis (reginae)* is perhaps the most popular in the group with white and carmine flowers.

Other orchids you might want to try are Habenarias and Spiranthes. They are occasionally available from suppliers.

Floating Plants for the Pool

The balance of life in a water garden is interdependent: water lilies, other water plants, and goldfish flourish in a balanced union. (See Chap. 11.)

If you have fish in the pool, some floating and submerged plants must be added to keep them healthy. Furthermore, water lilies are much more beautiful with a background of accessory plants:

A bunch of water plants decorate this pond: upper right (Snowflake), lower right (Water poppy) and at left (Floating heart). (Clint Bryant photo)

Azolla caroliniana. Mosslike plant with tiny scalloped leaves; a dainty addition to the pool. Spreads quickly and forms a water carpet of dull green to dark red in the sunlight.

Duckweed *(Glemna minor).* Another tiny plant with oval leaves. Grows rapidly and can be a nuisance, so use it sparingly.

Eoldea. A free-growing oxygenator, with slender foliage that grows underwater. Pinch off old growth to control. Thrives in sunlight.

Salvina. Heart-shaped, tiny, and hairy leaves. Grows vigorously, and will soon cover sections of water with a lovely velvetlike carpet.

Water hyacinth *(Eichornia crassipes).* A floating plant with inflated leafstalks and erect leaves. Lovely flowers are violet with a yellow eye and are produced in clusters on spikes. Wind can weaken them, so plant hyacinth in a wooden frame where they will be contained. *E. azurea* is a species with purplish-blue flowers.

Water chestnut *(Trapa natans).* A floating annual herb with toothed triangular leaves in clusters. Floats by means of swollen hollow stems 2 to 4 inches long. Flowers are small and white.

Water lettuce *(Pistia stratiotes).* Floats on the surface of the pool. Has trailing, long, and hairlike roots, and resembles garden lettuce. Roots should be in soil for best growth. A pretty addition.

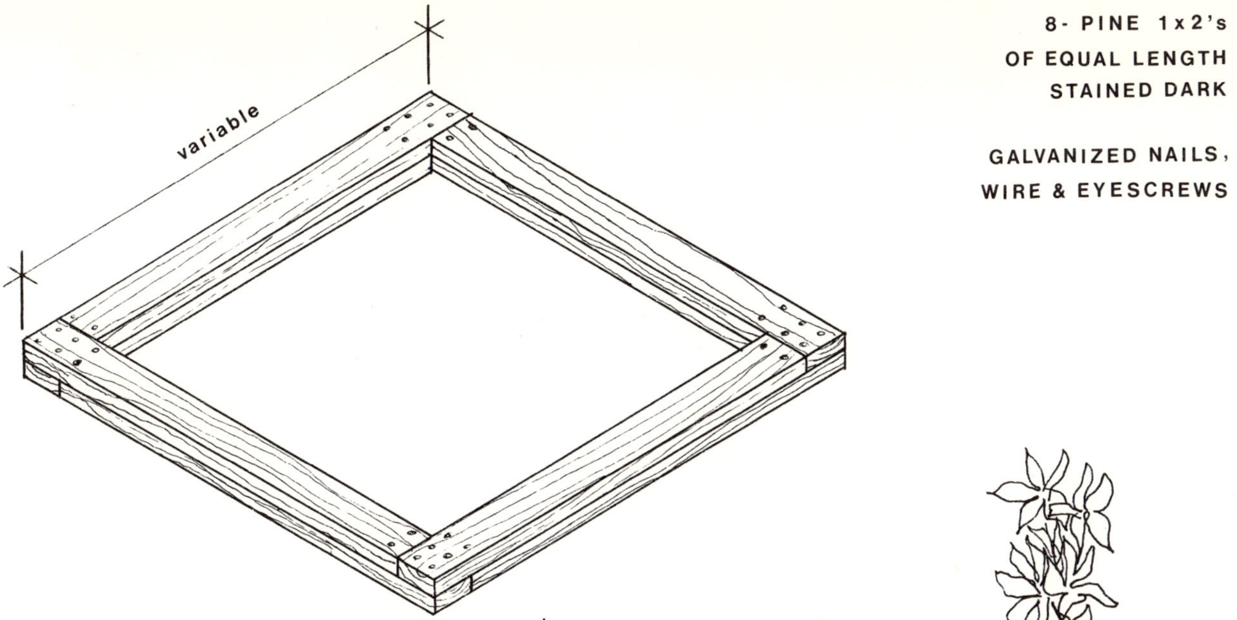

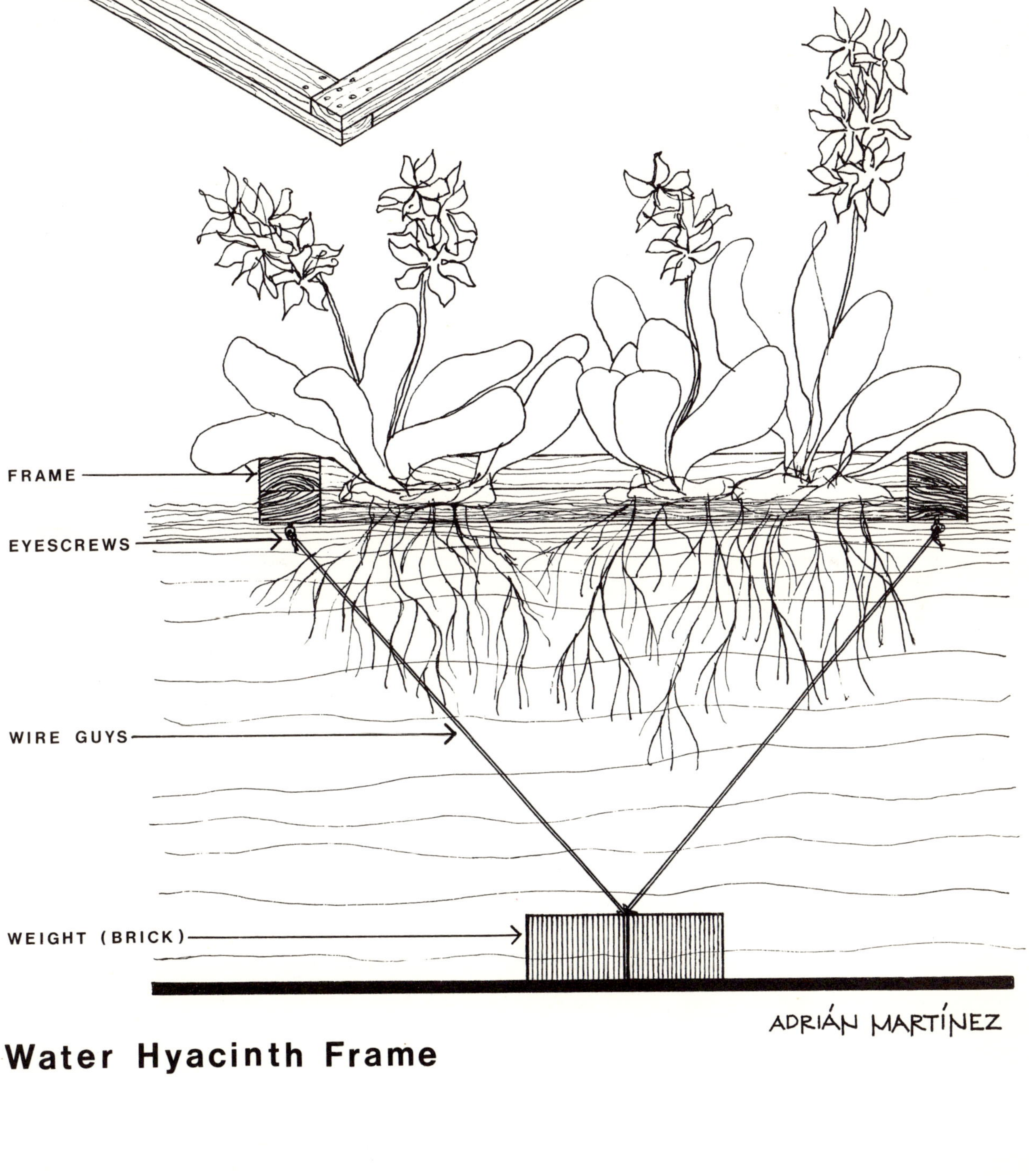

Water Hyacinth Frame

Water-poppy *(Hydrocleys nymphoides)*. A lovely aquatic with small yellow flowers. Resembles a miniature water lily and blooms all summer. Plants thrive in only 3 inches of water. In small pools where lilies can't be grown this is an excellent substitute.

Water-snowflake *(Nymphoides indicum)*. A pretty little plant with 1-inch flowers resembling a flake of snow. Does well in 3- to 6-inches of water. Floating-hearts *N. peltatum* has bright yellow fringed flowers. Needs moist soil.

Arrowhead *(Sagittaria graminea)*. Grassy leaves. Grows freely in water. From same genus as Border Sagittaria. Good oxygenator.

Water violet *(Hottonia palustris)*. Charming plant with loose spikes of mauve flowers. Leaves are submerged; flowers produced on leafless stems above water in early summer. Place in shallow water.

Water hawthorn *(Aponogeton distachyus)*. A winter-flowering aquatic that needs about 8 inches of water. Has little white flowers and a tuberous rootstalk with floating narrow leaves.

Ludwigia. A good submerged plant for shallow water; foliage floats on surface of water. Bears round, glossy, and green leaves, and can grow to 3 feet. Keep in bounds by cutting.

Water poppies accented with Cyperus are part of a pool scene. (Clint Bryant photo)

10. Water Lilies and Lotus

Anyone with a garden pool will want to have some water lilies. Like orchids and roses, they are hard to resist. Lotus plants have allure too, and no doubt they will also be included in the water garden.

The most colorful and well-known of all genera in the water lily family is the genus called Nymphaea. Extensive hybridization has been done in this group to produce flowers of magnificent shape and color. There are hundreds of varieties and it seems each one is more beautiful than the other.

The plants are divided into two classes: the hardy lilies, with medium to large-sized flowers and the exotic tropicals with larger and more colorful flowers. Almost all tropical lilies are fragrant; some open by day and others at night. Colors range from white to pink, yellow to red in the hardies; in the tropicals we find the breath-taking blue and purple hues.

Some outstanding hybrids (the word is used interchangeably with variety here) in the hardy group were raised by M. Bory Latour Marliac towards the end of the last century. In the tropical lilies, Mr. George Pring of the Missouri Botanic Gardens has raised some superlative varieties.

Once planted in a rich soil in a sunny location, lilies require little care. They do not need to be watered or pampered. The tropicals are somewhat more difficult to get started but once growth is under way, they, like the hardies, need little care.

The foliage of water lilies grows continuously through summer

NYMPHAEA
(water lily)

and feedings in June and July will produce heavy growth and abundant flowers.

Hardy Water Lilies

The hardy water lilies bloom during the day, and generally the flowers float on the water, although several varieties thrust blossoms above the water.

The plants have fleshy rootstocks (rhizomes) and are shipped from nurseries in damp moss and oiled paper in April or May. Try to plant them as soon as possible; leaving them in their boxes for even a few days lessens the chance of their becoming established quickly. If the tubers get too dry from delayed planting, put them in tepid water for a day or two before planting. However, don't just plunge them into a pool freshly filled with water; deep and cold water is often fatal. Be sure the water has been standing at least 2 weeks so that it has been warmed by the sun.

Tubers can go directly into a sandy loam at the bottom of the pool, but container growing is the best way to cultivate plants. It eliminates a great deal of fuss and bother, and in boxes they can be moved easily. There are many different kinds of containers but wood ones are the most popular. (Use pine, not redwood; redwood turns water black and may kill plants.) A simple box can be made from 1 x 12-inch stock; make the container 1 foot square and 1 foot deep, and plant one lily to a box.

To keep the box from floating, nail a batten across the bottom or place a rock on top of the box, *not on top of the plant.* Elevate all planting tubs and boxes a few inches from the floor of the pool. Put them on bricks or stones; it is easy to clean under boxes when necessary.

Container growing also makes it possible to control the growth of Lilies; many can go rampant in the bottom of a pool and crowd out others. In a container, the food supply is limited, so it gives some of the weaker varieties a chance to grow.

The ideal container is about 20 inches square and 10 inches deep. There are variations, but anything larger than 24 inches is a waste of space. A tub or half barrel is an excellent container.

Put water lilies in a good loamy soil. Do not use leaf mold in the mix; it will foul the pool as it decomposes. Fertilize plants every

Soil is added to tub.

Fertilizer mixed with the soil.

*Hole dug for water lily,
sand added to keep soil in place.*

*Planted water lily
ready to be put into pool.*

spring and again in July. To feed the lilies put a balanced fertilizer (available from Lily specialists) in a paper bag or a cloth pouch and poke it into the soil around the plant (or use pellet-type fertilizer). Mix it into the bottom 2 inches of soil. Never use fresh manure; it sours the soil. And, never add lime to soil, but do use a few tablespoons of bone meal.

Winter Care

Most gardeners let hardy lilies rest in their containers at the bottom of the pool through winter; below the frost line (in most parts of the country) they will safely survive. If the frost line in your region is below 24 inches (call your local agricultural station and ask them), place boards over the pool, with leaves on top for further insulation, or winter hardies indoors.

To winter indoors, take hardies from the planting box, wash them, and store in clean, barely moist sand. Remember that rats and mice feast on Lily roots, so keep the stored plants in containers or bags with air holes.

The following water lilies are a sampling of the many hardy kinds available. To simplify the descriptions the plants are listed by color. If I have failed to include your favorite it is a matter of space, not choice.

Pink Varieties:

Amabilis. Tulip-shaped; good bright pink. Bloom is erect.
Esmeraldo. Rose-pink and white flowers; star-shaped.
Fire Crest. Almost red; early spring bloomer.
Formosa. A true pink and a terrific bloomer.
Helen Fowler. Light pink; fragrant. Flowers well above water.
Laydekeri Purpurata. Rose-colored with purple tones.
Leviathan. Large deep pink flowers.
Lustrous. Rose-pink with silvery sheen and yellow stamens.
Marguerite La Place. Soft rose-lilac blooms.
Marliac Rosea. Large cup shape; free bloomer.
Mrs. Richmond. Deep pink with lilac tint. A rare variety.
Morning Glory. Large blossoms; shell-pink.
Neptune. Pink blossoms and garnet stems. Striking.
Rene Gerard. Deep rose color; star-shaped.

Rose Arvey. Bright cerise-pink blossoms; sweetly scented.
Rosy Morn. A deep pink color; lovely shape.
Wilfron Gonnere. Handsome pink, full flowers.

White Varieties:
Albatross. A snow-white lily; large and very beautiful.
Gladstone. Pure white, cup-shaped flowers; very large.
Gonnere. Enormous snow-white blooms; free bloomer.
Hermine. A white lily; dainty and star-shaped blooms.
Richardsoni. Large snow-white blossoms with yellow stamens.
White Laydekeri. Snow-white with yellow center; dwarf lily. Excellent bloomer.

Yellow Varieties:
Chromatella. Bright yellow blossoms; a good bloomer.
Mexicana. A little beauty from Mexico. Can be a pest.
Pygmaea Helvola. Small yellow flowers that float on surface of water. A free bloomer.
Sunrise. Canary-yellow blossoms. Magnificent.

Red Varieties:
Arethusia. Deep dark-red blossoms.
Attraction. Garnet-red petals, white sepals, and rich mahogany stamens. Outstanding.
Conqueror. Deep crimson flowers shading to a deep pink.
Escarboucle. Intense red lily. Outstanding.
Gloriosa. Bright red flowers; early bloomer.
James Brydon. Rich rosy crimson blooms.
James Hudson. Rich red with mauve reflections; tulip-shaped blooms. A rare European variety.
Laydekeri Fulgens. Purplish-red flower; excellent bloomer.
Newton. Almost vermilion; large star-shaped flowers.
Picciola. Dark crimson blooms standing above the water; leaves spotted with red.
Red Laydekeri. Crimson flowers; good bloomer. Outstanding.
Sirius. Huge dark red flowers.
Sultan. Large cherry-red Lily; outer petals light rose. Good bloomer; exquisite.

Green Smoke. Martin E. Randig lily. (Van Ness Water Gardens photo by Clint Bryant)

Water lilies: Sunrise, 'Gonnere' *and* Gloriosa. (Van Ness Water Gardens photo by Clint Bryant)

Vesuve. Dark red; blooms profusely.

William Falconer. Darkest of all red lilies; not satisfactory in hot climate.

Miniature Pink Lilies:

Carmine Laydekeri (Lilacea). Carmine-pink colored; free blooming.

Joanne Pring. Rich deep pink blooms.

Mme. Maurice Laydekeri. Small pink blooms.

Mary Patricia. Deep peach-blossom-pink blooms.

Maurice Laydekeri. Pink blooms; petal tops a mottled white.

Pink Laydekeri (Rosea). Pink blossoms; very small. Excellent bloomer; exquisite.

Planting Tropicals

These are the fabulous lilies you often see in conservatories, where they put on a special show of breath-taking color. The crisp, cool, green leaves and exquisite flowers are well known.

Tropicals are set out about a month to 6 weeks after the hardy varieties because the water must be somewhat warm, about 72 F. If possible place the tropicals so that 4 to 6 inches of water are above the crowns in the first month. Then lower them so that there is 8 to 10 inches of water above the crowns. Like the hardies, container culture is recommended for the tropicals.

These lilies are sold as growing plants, and the tubers are wrapped in earth or moss. Do not break the earth ball; plant it whole in the soil in the container or in the bottom of the pool. Hold the plants in place with a stone, and cover the soil with gravel. Be sure the roots are placed horizontally in the container, about 1 inch below the surface of the soil with the growing tip peeking from the soil. As mentioned, sprinkle the surface of the container with crushed stone or gravel to keep the soil in place under water.

Tropical water lilies are treated as annuals that die when winter comes. You can try to carry them over in a greenhouse, but I have

Top left: *Water lily* Sir Galahad *by Martin E. Randig.* (Van Ness Water Garden photo by Clint Bryant)

Bottom left: *Water lilies* Chromatella, *M. albida and* Gloriosa. (Van Ness Water Gardens photo by Clint Bryant)

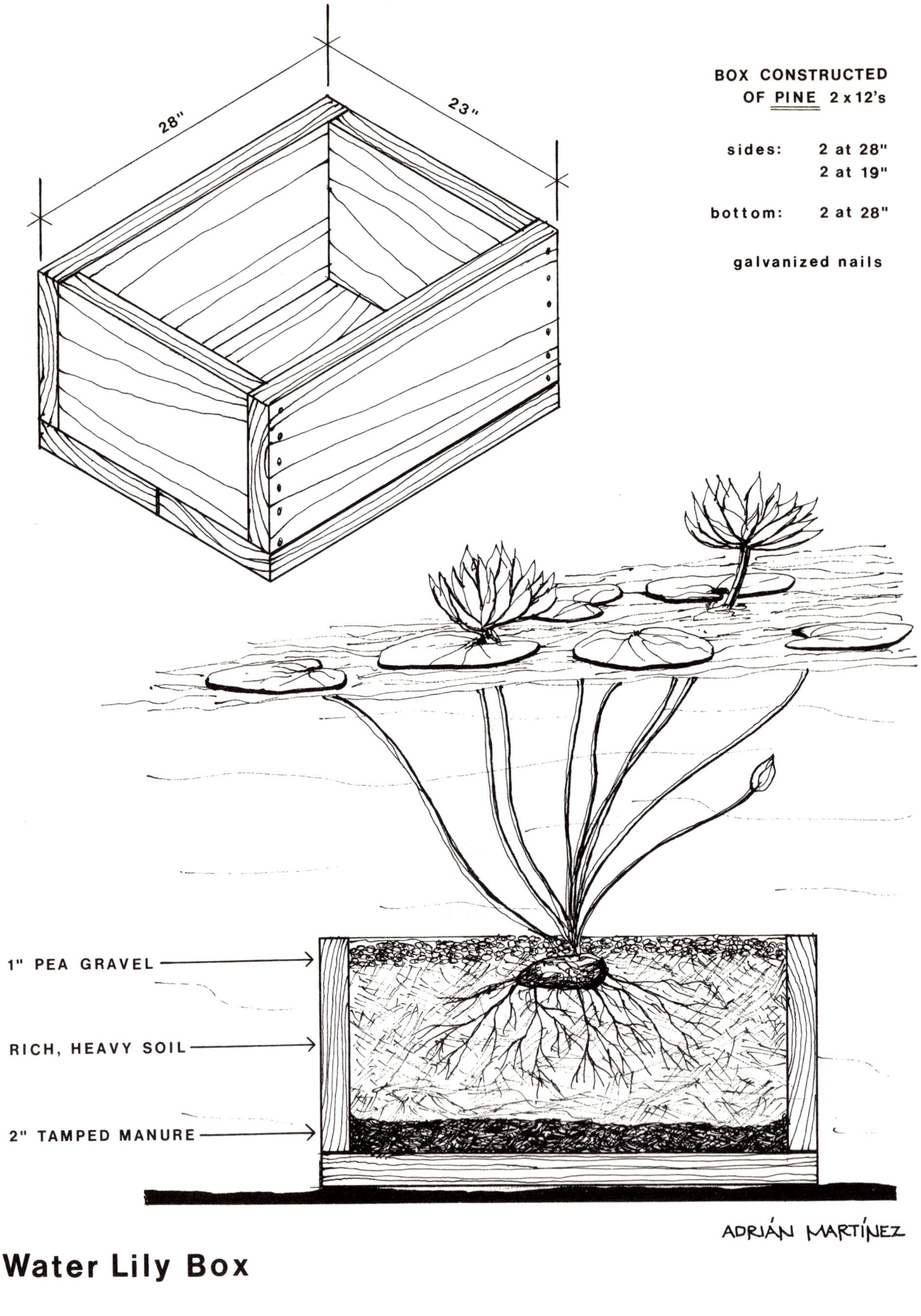

Water Lily Box

not been able to do so. I set out new ones in the pool each summer with a fresh supply of soil and fertilizer.

TROPICAL WATER LILIES

White Varieties:
Mrs. George Pring. Creamy-white blooms; open all day.
Ted Uber. Pure white, day-blooming lily. Outstanding.

Blue Varieties:
August Koch. Wisteria-violet petals; excellent plant. Good winter bloomer in greenhouse.
Blue Pygmaea or Colorata. Deep blue flowers; very fragrant.
Blue Triumph. Medium blue flowers of immense size.
Col. Lindbergh. Deep blue flowers; wide petals.
Mrs. Edward Whitaker. Lavender-blue flowers; open almost all day.
Pennsylvania. Large rich blue flowers; spicy fragrance. Free plant; vigorous bloomer.
Wm. Stone. Violet-blue, star-shaped blossoms.
Zanzibar Blue. Blue-purple flowers; very fragrant. Day bloomer.

Purple Varieties:
Francis B. Griffith. Dark purple; a leaf propagator.
Panama Pacific. Rich purple flowers; yellow stamens. Striking.
Royale Purple. Glowing royal-purple blooms.

Dark Blue Varieties:
Director Moore. Navy blue with yellow center. Outstanding.
Midnight. Dark violet, pointed petals. Beautiful.

Pink Varieties:
General Pershing. Orchid-pink flowers; open all day.
Pink Pearl. Silvery blossoms, pink with pure white throat.

Red Varieties:
American Beauty. A rose-red water lily.
Evelyn Randig. Rose-colored and red-toned blooms. Outstanding.

Water lilies: Ted Uber, Jamie Lu Skare *and* William C. Uber. (Van Ness Water Gardens photo by Clint Bryant)

Night Blooming Tropicals:
Missouri. White, semidouble flowers.
H. C. Haarstick. Vivid red, shading to rose-pink blossoms.
Mrs. John A. Wood. Maroon-red lily; beautiful.
Mrs. George Hitchcock. Large rose-pink flowers; good bloomer.
Mrs. Emily Hutchings. Pink blossoms; good bloomer.

Tropical Lilies (by Martin E. Randig):
Ted Uber. Pure white flowers; excellent bloomer.
Evelyn Randig. Deep magenta-rose blossoms; fragrant.
Mr. Martin E. Randig. Magenta-rose blooms; long petals.
Leopardess. Cobalt-blue flowers; excellent grower.

Margaret Randig. Large sky-blue blossoms; outstanding.

Mrs. Martin E. Randig. Dark purple-blue flowers; sepals dark rose-pink.

Enchantment. Deep salmon-rose blooms; free flowering. Excellent bloomer.

Leading Lady. Huge peach-pink blooms; strong grower.

Green Smoke. Chartreuse shading to light blue tips; fragrant.

Trail Blazer. Dark, starry, yellow flowers; prolific bloomer.

Yellow Dazzler. Rich chrome-yellow flowers; good bloomer. Outstanding.

Afterglow. Deep talisman to orange in color.

Golden Fascinator. Gold-tipped talisman blooms. Exquisite.

Golden West. Light apricot blooms; beautiful.

Star Lilies:

Blue Star. Clear blue blossoms; stands above the water.

Orchid Star. Orchid blossoms; outstanding.

Pink Star. Soft pink blossoms; good bloomer.

Water lily Louella G. Uber, *a tropical new lily for 1970 by Van Ness Water Gardens*

Purple Star. Violet-blue blossoms; yellow stamens tipped with blue; outstanding.
Red Star. Deep red blooms.
Rose Star. Rose-purple flowers; excellent bloomer.
White Star. Large white flowers; pointed petals.

Water Lotus—Genus Nelumbo

These incredible plants command interest and admiration because their beautiful large flowers on tall stems are truly spectacular. A native of India, the lotus was sacred to Hindus, who considered it the most exalted flower. The plant also appeared as a basic motif in Persian and Assyrian art.

The lovely, silvery, blue-green leaves are often 30 inches in diameter, and plants bloom from the end of June to the end of August. The foliage (like shallow bowls) does not have the customary notch at the junction of stem and leaf. The flowers sometimes reach 12 inches in diameter, and most are fragrant. They open just slightly the first day, close, then open again the following morning, and remain open for several hours before they close again. On the third day they open full.

Plants grow quickly, and good-sized roots may bloom in the first season; satisfactory flowering occurs in the second season. Lotus are hardy so long as the roots are below the frost line (about 18 inches of water). In their containers they will be perfectly safe through winter, provided the ice does not touch the crown of the plant.

Plant lotus in the spring when warm weather has started. Be careful not to break the growing tip of the tuber. For best growth put plants in a wooden tub, box, or half barrel. Use large containers at least 24 inches in diameter; if roots strike the corner of a planter they may die.

To plant lotus, make a hole in a container filled to within 4 inches of the rim with soil and fertilizer. Place one root horizontally in the trench, and cover with 2 inches of soil; leave about 0.5 inch of the growing tip exposed. Put a flat stone on the covered root, and add more sand, being careful not to touch the growing tip. Put one pound of fertilizer in the bottom of the tub or pool. Be sure the lotus is covered with 3 to 4 inches of water, and repot plants every other

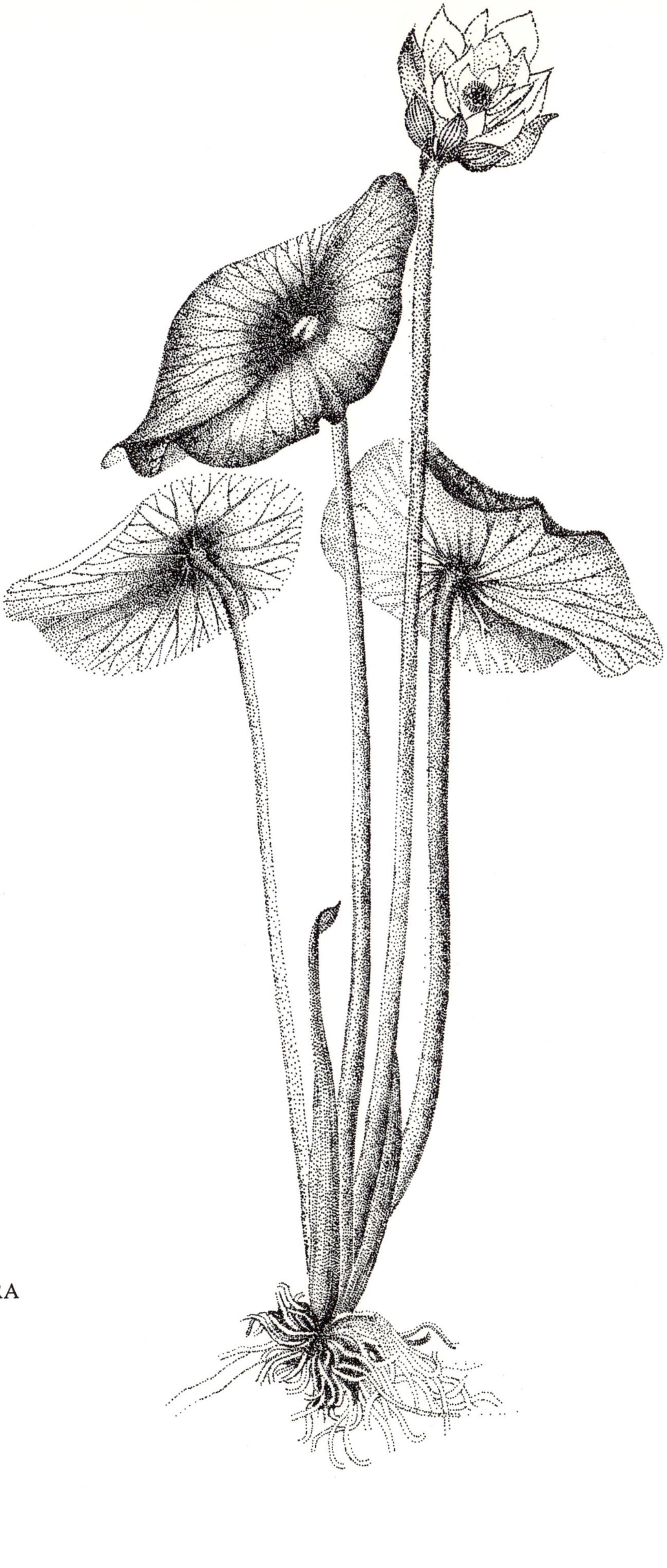

NELUMBO NUCIFERA
(water lotus)

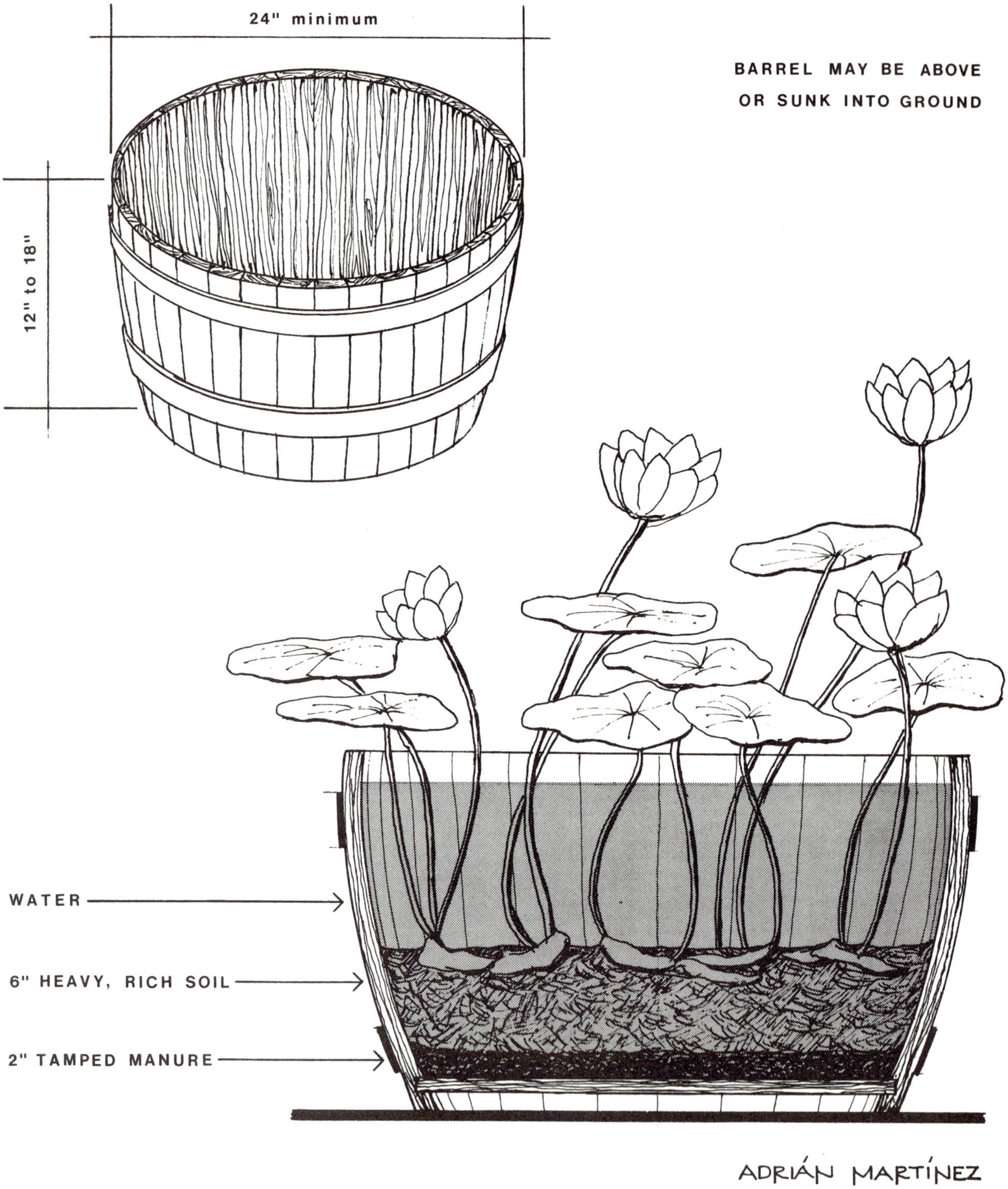

Lotus Barrel

year in a fresh supply of soil and fertilizer. (Without feeding lotus will not grow.)

Lotus stock is generally limited at most nurseries, so order before May.

Botanical classes of lotuses (Nelumbo) change frequently, and there are several disagreements among authorities about names. For a simple workable class we list plants as follows:

Nelumbo lutea (American lotus). Lovely light yellow flowers.

N. lutea var. *flavescens.* Smaller blooms with red spots at base of petals.

N. nucifera (Asiatic lotus). Handsome pink flowers with many varieties:

- var. *rosea plenum:* large, pink, double blooms.
- var. *pekinensis rubra* (rosea): rosy-red flowers.
- var. *pygmaea alba:* dwarf, with white blooms.

N. Shiroman. A beautiful white double Lotus; huge flowers. Free blooming.

N. Kinshiren. A white-flowering plant with touches of rose color.

Plant Protection

You will find that water lilies are amazingly free from insect attacks and disease problems. Because they are in water and sunlight they are vigorous, healthy plants, rarely bothered with the problems that their earth-borne relatives may suffer. However, the following is information about the few insects and fungi that occasionally attack plants.

Aphids. Round-bodied pests that are easily seen. They appear on leaf stems and eventually move on to the leaves and suck vital plant juices. However, they are easy to eliminate: wash them off with a fine spray from the garden hose.

Caddis flies. These little devils feed on the roots, buds, and leaves of just about anything that grows in water. The best control is to have goldfish in the pool; the caddis fly larvae is their favorite food.

Leaf roller. A larval pest that eats leaf edges and can cause considerable damage to plants unless caught early. Control is simple: pinch off infested leaves or cut away rolled-up leaf edges.

Leaf beetle. This is a small beetle that hibernates in poolside vegetation. In June, it lays ovate eggs on leaf surfaces. The larvae feed

The exotic lotus leaves and flowers add the charm of the Orient to any pool; here, yellow and red Shiroman are featured. (Photo courtesy Van Ness Water Gardens, by Clint Bryant)

on leaves, and their work can soon be seen. Goldfish is the best control; they eat the larvae and eggs.

Fungus occasionally attacks water lilies and causes dark patches on the leaves. The best remedy is to remove the affected foliage immediately and burn it. Another fungus attacks stems, causing a blackening and rotting away of the growth. Copper sulfate is the usual remedy, but use it with utmost caution: 0.5 ounce placed in a small cloth bag for a pool that holds 2000 gallons of water. Pull the bag around the pool until the crystals have dissolved.

Fortunately, fungus diseases are very rare in the small garden pool.

11. Goldfish in the Pool

For added interest and fascinating viewing in the water garden you might want to have goldfish, to create a balanced garden of plants, water, and fish.

In a well-stocked pool the water cannot take in enough oxygen by surface evaporation to replace that used by the fish, so water plants that give off oxygen are necessary. Fish, as they take in oxygen from water, give off carbon dioxide; water plants convert it into the manufacture of plant tissue.

Before putting fish into the water be sure that it is suitable for them. As mentioned in Chap. 3, a newly built concrete pool must be filled with water several times over a period of weeks before the water in it can accommodate fish or plants. All alkaline in the water must be gone, or the plants and fish will be harmed. Oxygenating water plants should also be in place a few weeks before adding fish to the pool.

Be sure the pool is at least 20 inches deep for fish. In shallow pools they do not live long, and if you have raccoons in the area be prepared to lose some of the fish.

Goldfish

Centuries ago the Chinese recognized the beauty of goldfish. From the tenth to the thirteenth centuries, during the Sung dynasty, goldfish were kept as pets; Japanese breeders started to cultivate them on a grand scale around 1700.

These small members of the carp family have been bred so extensively that there are hundreds of varieties. Those suitable for

COMET (A) CALICO (C) SHUBUNKIN (E) COMMON (G)
FANTAIL (B) VEILTAIL (D) BLACK MOOR (F) KOI (H)

outdoor pools include Comets, (one of the fastest and most graceful, with large fins and tails), Shubunkin (multitudes of colors), Moors (a small pretty fish of velvety black), fantailed Calicos (mottled coloring), and the common goldfish. All will survive in pools in cold-winter regions. Beautiful fish like the Oranda and Lionhead are fragile and not hardy enough to live in an outdoor pool through winter.

Common goldfish varieties sell from 35 cents to 5 dollars, often exceed 20 inches in length, and may live for twenty years in a suitable environment. Another type of fish, developed by the Japanese and called "Koi," is also available. They come in many different color varieties and are excellent outdoor-pool fish. They do best in temperate regions and in water over 36 inches deep that doesn't freeze solidly in winter. They are bottom feeding fish and do best in running-water pools or ponds.

At first, try the common, inexpensive varieties—(there are so many); you then can try some of the more exotic kinds.

Feeding and Care

Unlike household pets that occasionally need pampering, goldfish thrive on neglect. Do not overfeed them, even if you think they are hungry; in a pool well-balanced with plants they have more than enough food. Insects and their eggs and larvae are goldfishes' diet, but if you enjoy feeding the fish and seeing them come to the surface of the water for their meal—and they can be trained to do this—give them packaged food, but occasionally and sparingly. Remember that surplus food will decompose and foul the water, harming the fish.

In a pool not yet established you will have to feed the fish packaged food. Give them only as much food as they can eat in 5 minutes, and feed them every other day.

Do not worry about water temperature; in summer it will be sufficiently warm, in fall the water cools somewhat, and in winter in most areas it will freeze. But since the temperature change is gradual it does not disturb the fish.

Water ranging from 50 to 80°F is suitable for most goldfish, although some prefer an ideal of 60 to 70°F. They can endure winter under ice but will not be active or grow during the cold months. They will need no food at all while the pool is frozen over. When the ice begins to melt and the fish start to move around again, resume feeding until water plants are established. Once ice forms don't attempt to break it or feed the fish. Breaking the ice shocks the fish (like hitting a person on the head with a rock).

When you clean the pool you disturb the balance of nature. Natural food for the fish is gone, and new water is deadly because of its chemical content. While the pool is being cleaned and the water properly ages for several days, keep the fish in a wide-mouth, 5-gallon pickle jar full of water from the pool.

When the pool is ready for fish submerge the jar in the pool, almost to its rim. Leave it there so that water temperatures can equalize slowly. Then fully submerge and tip the jar so that the fish can swim into the pool. Until a natural food supply builds up again—about a month—you will have to use prepared foods for the fish. (There are many at suppliers.) Feed them only a small amount each day; remember that excess food will decompose and contaminate the water for plants and fish.

Goldfish will keep a pool relatively free of mosquito larvae.

Ordering Goldfish

Today goldfish may be shipped easily in polyethylene bags; you can be reasonably sure they will arrive in good condition. (If possible place your orders in spring.) When the goldfish arrive leave them in the polyethylene bag and float them in the pool for about an hour (keep the bag fully inflated.) This equalizes the temperature of the water in the bag and the water in the pool.

SOURCES FOR WATER PLANTS

Some water plants are available at local nurseries in early spring. The majority of them, however—water lilies and lotus in many varieties—are best ordered from suppliers specializing in these plants. These companies offer handsome color catalogs; write for them. It is the best way to select plants of your preference.

Van Ness Water Gardens 2460 North Euclid Avenue Upland, Calif. 91786	Catalog available; a fine supply of water lilies and other aquatics. Supplies, pools, goldfish.
Slocum Water Gardens 1101 Cypress Gardens Rd. Winter Haven, Fla. 33880	
Paradise Gardens Bedford at May St. Whitman, Mass. 02382	
Three Springs Fisheries 120 Main Road Lilypons, Md. 21717	Catalog available; Excellent source for water lilies and supplies. Goldfish.
William Tricker Inc. Box 398 Saddle River, N.J. 07458 or Box 7845 Independence, Ohio 44131	Catalog available; Water lilies and other aquatic plants. Supplies.
S. Scherer & Sons Waterside Rd. Northport, N.Y. 11768	Water lilies
Michigan Bulb Co. Grand Rapids, Mich. 49502	Water lilies and supplies.

WHERE TO BUY POOLS, FOUNTAINS, ORNAMENTS, STATUARY, PUMPS

Many containers for pools are at local nurseries and garden centers. Mail order suppliers also furnish pools, fountains and statuary. Write for catalogs.

Aqualite Pool Co. 430 Bedford St. Whitman, Mass. 02382	Molded pools.
Little Giant Pump Co. 3810 North Tulsa Oklahoma City, Okla. 73112	Pumps and fountain kits.
Kenneth Lynch & Sons Wilton, Conn. 06897	Excellent source for fountains and statuary of all kinds.
Rain Jet Corp. 301 S. Flower Burbank, Calif. 91503	Fountain kits.
Tuscany Studios 548 North Wells St. Chicago, Ill. 60610	Statuary of all kinds.
Bello-Groppi Studio 421 W. Wisconsin Ave. Chicago, Ill. 60614	Stone fountains of all kinds.
Aldocraft Co. 210 Fifth Ave. New York, N.Y. 10010	Statuary, fountains.

WHERE TO BUY LIGHTING FIXTURES FOR POOLS AND FOUNTAINS

Shalda Lighting Products, Inc.
P.O. Box 507
Burbank, Calif. 91503

Loran, Inc.
P.O. Box 911
Redlands, Calif. 92373

Rain Jet Corp.
301 S. Flower St.
Burbank, Calif. 91503

BOOKS FOR WATER GARDENERS

Water in The Garden by Douglas Bartrum, John Gifford Publishers, London W.C. 2, 1968.

Garden Pools, Water lilies and Goldfish by G. L. Thomas, Jr. Van Nostrand Publishing Co. Princeton, N.J. 1958.

The Book of the Garden Pond by George F. Hervey & Jack Hems, Faber & Faber, London, 1970. (First published by Stanley Paul & Co. Ltd. 1958.)